Delia Emma Rawlings

Delia Emma Rawlings

What Instrument Shall I Play?

What Instrument Shall I Play?

Text by Nicholas Ingman

Illustrations by Bernard Brett

Ward Lock Limited · London

Acknowledgements

The photographs of students playing various instruments are of members of the School Orchestra at Reigate Grammar School, by kind permission of the Headmaster, Mr. H. M. Balance, and with the co-operation of the Music Instructor, Mr. M. A. Ferns.

Photographs by courtesy of Barnaby's Picture Library, Boosey & Hawkes Group, BBC Pictorial Publicity, Camera Clix Inc., Mary Evans Picture Library, Mrs. S. Fawcus, Barbara Graham Management, Mark Gudgeon, Greater London Council, Dezo Hoffman, Ibbs & Tillett, National Gallery, Oxford University Press, Pictorial Press Ltd., Radio Times Hulton Picture Library, S.K.R. Photos International Ltd., Sotheby & Co., Syndication International Ltd., Topix, Victoria and Albert Museum, Reg Wilson, Van Wyck.

The author particularly wishes to thank Mr. Michael Hensor, Mr. Andrew Fairley, and Mr. Bram Gay for their very great help in checking the MS.

First published in Great Britain 1975
by Ward Lock Limited, 116 Baker Street,
London W1M 2BB

Designed by Andy Vargo

Text set in 11 on 12 pt Apollo
by Cox & Wyman Ltd, Fakenham, Norfolk

Printed and bound in Spain
by Editorial Fher S.A., Bilbao

By the same authors: THE STORY OF MUSIC

It should not be forgotten that some firms will supply instruments on hire, with an option to purchase after a certain period. This is a most useful service since it is always possible that the child may not 'get along' with the instrument he first chose and may wish to take up something else.

The approximate prices quoted in this table apply to the cheapest satisfactory instrument, suitable for the beginner, and are given here in order to provide the necessary basis for comparison of relative cost to the parent. It is, of course, understood that inflation may lead to price increases, but the costs should continue to bear the same relation to each other as is here shown. In every case the cost of a first-class, professional standard instrument will be very much higher than the prices given here.

Price	Instrument
£1–£5 $A3.50–$A17.50	Recorders, except bass recorder Ukulele Toy instruments Harmonica, Ocarina, Flageolet Bagpipe chanter
£10–£20 $A35–$A40	Violin Viola Xylophone Semi-toy portable organ Accordion Guitar Mandoline
£20–£30 $A70–$A100	Trumpet Cornet Bagpipes (Japanese) Bass recorder
£40–£50 $A140–$A175	Cello Clarinet B♭ trombone Banjo
£50–£60 $A175–$A210	Double bass Electric guitar Flute Timpani (each) Piano
£60–£80 $A210–$A280	Piccolo Flugelhorn
£90–£100 $A310–$A350	Oboe French horn (F) Electronic organ (small) Alto saxophone
£100–£200 $A350–$A700	Tenor saxophone B♭ Baritone Euphonium Pop- or jazz-group drums kit Bagpipes (Scottish)
£200–£400 $A700–$A1,400	Harp Bass clarinet Baritone saxophone Cor anglais Tuba Bassoon
£400–£500 $A1,400–$A1,750	Full double French horn Small electronic piano Sousaphone
Over £500 $A1,750	Contrabassoon Vibraphone Synthesizers

Contents

Four Trumpets—detail
from 'History of the
Coronation of James II'
by Francis Sandford

1 The World of Musical Instruments

The first and most important 'instrument' was the human voice. But ever since man discovered that singing was an agreeable alternative to talking, he has added to this idea by making sounds with objects—bits of wood, sea shells, tree trunks, reeds, bow strings.

Nobody knows what was the first instrument made by man, but it seems likely that it was some kind of drum— not a drum as we know it today, with skins and a round hollow body—but something which he *struck* to make a sound. Perhaps it was just two sticks banged together, perhaps it was one stick beating on a hollow tree trunk, perhaps it was one stone hitting another.

However primitive these first 'instruments' were they must have given primitive man the idea of different *sounds*— that is, sounds of different *pitch*, some high, some low, as well as sounds of different *quality*, some hard like striking two sticks together, some more mellow, like the booming noise of a hollowed-out tree trunk.

Thus, 'music' was born—the deliberate making of sounds of different pitch and different quality—and so was the whole world of musical instruments, which exist, even in their most complicated form, just to make sounds of different quality and pitch.

After the *percussion* instruments—that is, those that make their sound by being *struck*—the next development was probably those instruments that make their sound by air being blown over them or through them, the *wind* instruments.

Nobody knows for certain, of course, but in the distant past it may have happened that when the wind blew across the broken ends of the reeds growing near a river a kind of sighing noise was produced. Perhaps a caveman plucked a reed and blew across the end, imitating the wind, and discovering that he too could produce that sighing noise, which, if he blew harder, became a whistling note. Perhaps he accidentally discovered that if he blew across the open end of a hollow animal bone it produced an entirely new noise unlike anything he had ever heard before.

In this way primitive man may have taken the first step that was to lead to the invention of the recorder, the flute, the oboe, the bassoon, the clarinet, the saxophone—all of them today classified as wind instruments. But this would be beyond his imagination; nor could he have foreseen anything like the giant pipe organ, which is, after all, only a highly elaborate way of blowing wind down hollow tubes!

He did discover, however, another way of blowing down a tube. If he pressed his lips together when he blew, instead of just letting the air gush out through open lips, he found he produced an entirely different kind of sound. This time it was the *lips* that made the sound, the tube merely making the sound louder —or, to be a little more technical, it was the vibration of the lips that set in motion the column of air within the tube. And this led to the invention of all those instruments played with a cup mouthpiece—the trumpet, the cornet, the trombone, the tuba, the French horn—now called the 'brass' instruments.

Nor was that the end of man's experiments with disturbing the air. He discovered that if he found, or made, a flat

8

An eighteenth-
century musical
instrument workshop—
from Diderot's
Encyclopedia

oval-shaped piece of stone or bone or wood, pierced a hole at one end, tied a piece of thread through the hole and whirled the stone round his head, a most peculiar whirring sound was produced, caused by the stone spinning on its own axis as it was swung through the air. This instrument, called a bull roarer or thunder stick, is of very great antiquity, dating back at least 20,000 years. It is still in use today among primitive peoples like the aborigines of Australia or the natives of Central Africa as a means of contacting, or warding off, evil spirits. But, apart from this usage, it did not develop into a modern musical instrument, although the American composer, Henry Cowell, did write a work for two violins, viola, two cellos and two bull roarers! Perhaps one of these days someone will create an orchestra of a hundred bull roarers, all of different sizes and all

whirling through the air at different speeds!

The other great group of instruments is the *strings*. Again, nobody knows when or how these began. Undoubtedly their discovery, too, was accidental—perhaps a length of animal sinew was stretched tautly during the dismemberment of a carcass and when touched produced a twanging noise. How many thousands of years was it, one wonders, before this chance creation of a new sound developed into the deliberate stretching of a cord between two points in order that it should give out a pleasing noise when it was plucked by the fingers. But whenever and in whatever way it occurred, this was the beginning of violins, cellos, basses, guitars, banjos, harps and even the piano.

There is a famous cave drawing in the South of France, made some 25,000 years

Parts of the early
single-action harp,
showing the hook
mechanism—from
Diderot's Encyclopedia

ago, which is the oldest known picture of a musical instrument. It depicts a creature, part man, part bull (possibly a man dressed in an animal skin for some kind of ceremony) holding what might be either a bow with string attached or a hollow bone for blowing down—it is not certain which. But it could be considered to be evidence that at least 25,000 years ago man knew about the 'musical' qualities of a stretched string.

It is obvious that making music with instruments has been part of mankind's life for tens of thousands of years. It is not surprising, therefore, to find many legends surrounding the origins of different instruments. For instance, there is a story, at least two thousand years old, which tells of the occasion when Pan, the goat-footed god of the ancient Greeks, was chasing the nymph Syrinx through the woods. The gods, seeing that Pan was

gaining on her, decided to help by changing her into a bundle of reeds growing at the river bank. As Pan clasped the reeds to him and sighed in sorrow, he noticed that the reeds gave off a musical note—and thus was invented the Panpipes, or Syrinx, a series of tubes of various lengths bound together in a row and played by moving them across the mouth.

Another Greek god, Mercury, was said to have made the first lyre (a kind of small harp consisting of strings stretched across a sounding board) from a dried-out tortoise shell he found on the banks of the Nile.

Then again, according to Genesis 4, Jubal, the descendant of Cain, is supposed to be the 'father of all such as handle the harp and the organ'.

Today, the world of musical instruments is an immensely complicated one.

A modern musical
instrument workshop
(Boosey & Hawkes)

There are hundreds of different instruments ranging from the very simple such as the triangle—which nevertheless has its legitimate place in the symphony orchestra—to the electronic complexities of the Moog synthesizer, which can produce *billions* of different sounds.

All these instruments, in their various ways, either singly or in groups, can produce music. Some of them are hard to play and others are easy. Some are expensive to buy and others are cheap.

The world of musical instruments is a world of differences—not only in the instruments themselves, but in the way they are played and the ways in which they are formed into symphony orchestras, pop groups, jazz units, military and brass bands, school orchestras.

What instrument do you want to play? And in what kind of organization do you want to play it? The world of musical instruments is an exciting one in which boys and girls of all ages will find adventure and challenge and, in the end, a satisfaction which is unlike any other.

Musical instruments have always been an important feature of processions and parades

2 How Sounds Are Made

Sound travels by vibrations of the air; but there is rather more to sound than that, and although it is not necessary to get very technical about it, nor dig very deeply into the science of acoustics, as it is called, a certain understanding will help to achieve a greater appreciation of instruments and how they work.

Let us imagine a guitar string at rest on its instrument. No sound comes from it. But pluck it with the finger and immediately a sound is heard. Why? Because the string is vibrating—moving back and forth between its two fixed ends. There has to be a certain elasticity in the string to allow this—it could not happen, for instance, with a thick iron bar, or a broom handle. But the string is made of a material sufficiently thin, and is attached to the body of the instrument in such a way, that it can move backwards and forwards freely. Eventu-

ally, it will come to rest and the sound will cease.

But while it is moving back and forth, or vibrating, it is causing the air next to it also to move back and forth. And the air, like the string, springs back into its original position when the string does, having itself made the 'piece' of air next to it swing back and forth in a similar manner. The next piece of air also reacts similarly and so on and so on until the energy spends itself and the movement gets less and less and the sound fainter and fainter until eventually it cannot be heard at all.

One way of understanding this movement of the molecules of air is to imagine a number of round glass beads on a tray. Hit one bead and it will cannon into the next one, which will shoot off and hit another one, which in its turn . . . and so on, until all the beads become still.

The modern valve horn and its ancestor the 'natural' horn

What the horn would look like if it were 'opened out'

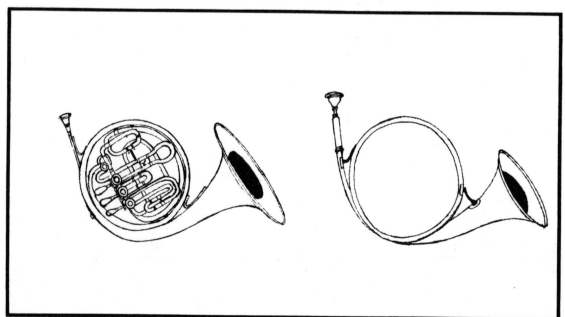

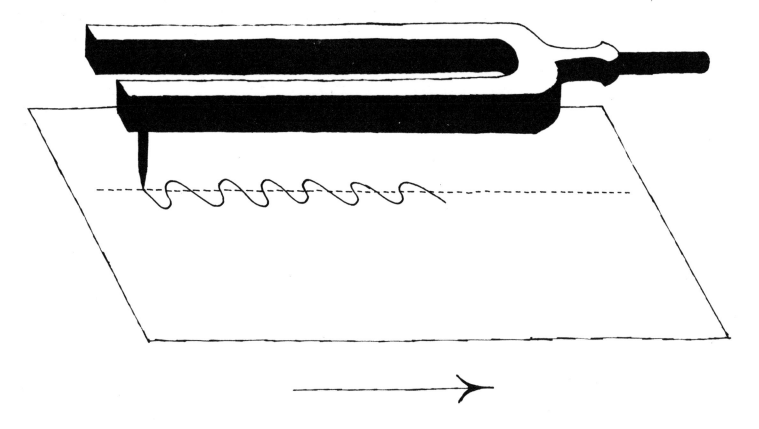

'Drawing' sound waves
by means of a pen
attached to a
tuning fork

A famous writer of the 1870s used to explain this to his pupils by making them stand in a row, one behind the other, each with his two hands on the shoulders of the student in front of him. 'I suddenly push A,' he wrote, 'then A pushes B and regains his upright position; B pushes C; C pushes D; D pushes E; each boy, after the transmission of the push, becoming himself erect. E, having nobody in front, is thrown forward. . . .'

The two points the writer was making were (i) how the sound was transmitted forward from the original source, and (ii) when it reached the end of the line, so to speak, there was some definite effect—i.e. the boy falling forward because there was nobody else for him to push—or, in other words, the sound finally reaching its objective—the ear, or the microphone. When the impulse reaches the ear, or microphone, it causes the ear drum, or microphone diaphragm, to move back and forth. In the case of the ear this causes a reaction in the nerve leading to the brain which causes the listener to 'hear' the music. The microphone converts the impulse into an electric current and passes it via a wire to wherever it has to go—a loudspeaker, or recording machine.

The sound waves eventually die out,

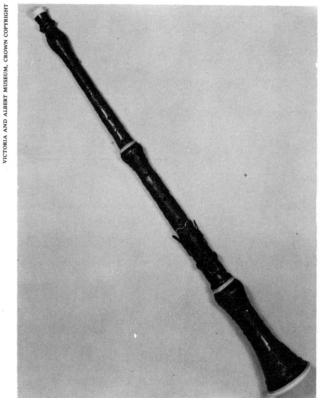

200-year-old carved boxwood oboe

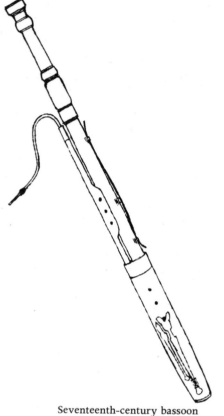

Seventeenth-century bassoon

as has been said. Or to be more strictly accurate, they diminish to such a low level that neither the human ear nor even the most sensitive recording instrument can detect them. But theoretically they are still continuing—on and on and on for ever, past the outer planets and into what science fiction writers call 'deep space'. Think of a pebble dropped into a pool. If it is a small pool you can see the ripples eventually reach the water's edge. But if it is a very large pool they *seem* to die out although sometimes you can still see fronds below the surface moving slowly backwards and forwards.

Going back to our imaginary guitar for a moment, you will see that the strings are of different thicknesses and you will notice that the thicker the string the lower the note it produces. This is because the *pitch* of the sound depends on how *fast* the string swings back the forth and makes the surrounding air swing back and forth. The number of times the string (or air) moves back and forth in

a second is called the *frequency* of the sound (the word 'frequency' merely means 'how often'). If it moves a relatively few times in a second, it is a 'low frequency'; if many times, a 'high frequency'. And a low frequency produces a low note, and a high frequency a high note.

The lowest note the human ear can detect is about 16 vibrations per second —and that is so low that it is a rumble rather than a note. It is the sort of noise produced by the largest pipe on the largest church organ—you can feel it shake the ground rather than hear it— and you certainly couldn't sing it. The lowest note on a piano has a frequency of 27·5 vibrations per second, and the highest note on the piccolo has 5,274 vibrations per second.

The human ear can go well above this and can detect a sound of vibrations up to 16,000 per second. Exceptionally sharp ears can get up to 20,000, but after that the human ear fails to hear anything.

Mediaeval great bass shawm—an early member of the oboe family

How sound impulses are passed through the air. The first molecule pushes the second molecule, which pushes the third, and so on. A graphic illustration from an 1875 treatise on Sound

Animals and insects have much sharper hearing and can go well beyond 20,000. There are dog whistles, for instance, pitched above the 20,000 frequency range, which are quite inaudible to humans but which the dog can hear perfectly. There is a story that a certain famous pop group included a high-pitch dog whistle in one of its recordings, so that when the record was played, any dog which happened to be in the room pricked up its ears and stared expectantly at the record player, to the complete astonishment of the humans present who couldn't imagine why the dog was reacting that way.

Not all available frequencies are used by musical instruments since many of them wouldn't be heard. Another, less obvious, reason is that the average human ear cannot detect any difference between notes a few vibrations apart. Another factor is the impracticality of making an instrument with, say, 20,000 keys!

So all musical instruments fall more or less within the same 120 different frequencies. A grand piano has 88 notes, a very large organ has more, both above and below those of the piano. All instruments keep within these 120 frequencies, though the human voice, the trombone, other wind instruments, the synthesizer and members of the string family can play intermediate steps. Normally, when instruments wander from these fixed 120 notes they are said to be 'out of tune'.

The various instruments produce their sounds in one of three ways: (i) by being struck (like a drum, or a vibraphone, or bells), (ii) by a string being set in motion by bowing (violin, cello, etc.), by plucking (guitar, banjo, harp), or striking (piano, zither), or (iii) by a column of air in a tube being set in motion by vibrating a reed (clarinet, saxophone, oboe), or by vibrating the lips (trumpet, trombone, tuba), or by blowing across the edge of a hole (flute, piccolo).

3 Why Different Instruments Produce Different Sounds

We know that different instruments can be made to produce their vibrations in different ways—plucking a string, blowing down a tube and so on. But why does this make them sound different?

It is useful to know a little about this because it is the quality, or *timbre*, of the various instruments that gives them their individuality—and this is tremendously important to anyone who plays an instrument. If they all sounded alike, much of that which pleases the ear, and everything that makes for the richness of the sound of an orchestra, would be lost.

The first thing that makes for this difference is, of course, the basic method of making the sound—the blown tube, the plucked string—so that sounds produced by one can never be mistaken for the other. But this is only the starting point of the differences.

The next factor is the method of increasing the loudness—of amplifying the rather small and dull sound of the actual vibration. For instance, stringed instruments use a hollow wooden body which increases the volume of sound. Wind instruments—both wood and brass—use a tube to amplify the basic sound. Percussion (struck) instruments of the xylophone or vibraphone type often use long metal tubes suspended under the bars to amplify the sound made when the bars are struck. The hollow bodies of drums serve the same purpose; indeed, without the body a drum head would make hardly any sound at all.

In addition, of course, the sounds thus produced can be made louder or softer by the degree of force put into producing them. A tone is made louder because a string is plucked or bowed with more force, or because a drum is hit harder, or because a wind player blows harder. But the energy way of making more volume is effective only if the resonating power is there to build on.

Thus we have accounted for *pitch*—whether the note is high or low—and *volume*—whether it is loud or soft. But equally important is the *quality*, or *timbre*, of the sound produced, for it is this which makes one instrument sound different from another.

There are several reasons for this difference in quality in addition to the basic method of producing the sound. First, there is the shape and size of the instrument; secondly, there are details of construction, like the *f* holes on a string instrument; and lastly the material of which the instrument is made.

The size of an instrument obviously has a lot to do with how it sounds and this matter of size is complementary to the size of the actual sound-producing medium. Although a cello is roughly the same *size* as a tuba, one could never be mistaken for the other. In fact, the very top notes of the cello sound very much like the bottom notes of the violin or viola, except to an expert ear.

Size, therefore, is only part of it. The viola has longer strings than the violin; the cello has longer strings than the viola; the string bass has longer strings than the cello. It is the length and thickness of the strings combined with the size of the instrument which determines the basic quality, the size of the instrument being the necessary 'support' for the longer, stronger, thicker strings. In electronically amplified versions of the cello

An old 6-string Italian mandola—a member of the lute family

Stringed instruments of
the early seventeenth
century

and bass the bodies have been dispensed with altogether, their amplifying function being replaced by microphones.

The sound holes of a string instrument have a lot to do with its sound. Without these, string instruments would sound very dull. Their purpose is to regulate the amount of air in the body of the instrument. Called f holes because of their shape, they are the result of centuries of experimentation. The earliest stringed instruments had round sound holes, as the guitar still does today. Then came twin openings shaped like the letter c with their backs to each other and these were followed by inverted pairs, like this ς, which were the forerunners of the modern f hole.

But the most important reason for differences in sound quality is that the sounds are made up not of one frequency but of several, all mixed together. These 'extra' sounds are called harmonics or overtones, and there is an almost infinite

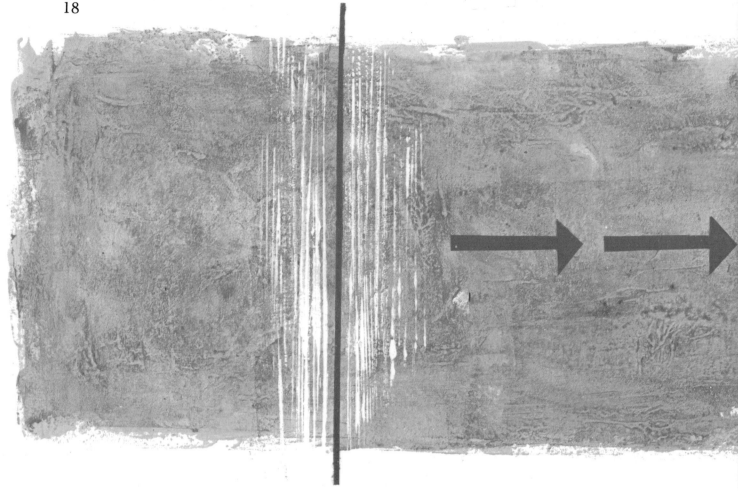

number of them. It is the presence of these additional frequencies along with the basic one (which determines the pitch) which gives the sound its special and different quality. Each instrument, because of its structure, size and so on, has its own particular 'mixture'. Thus, the 'mixture' which is produced by middle C on the piano, is completely different from the 'mixture' produced by middle C on the trombone.

To express this more scientifically, we can say that a string or column of air, set in motion, vibrates not only as a whole, but in parts. Figure 1 in the drawing herewith shows how a string (or column of air) vibrates as a whole—this gives the fundamental, or basic note. Figure 2 shows that it *also* vibrates in halves, which produces a harmonic an octave higher and much softer than the basic note, with which it combines. Figure 3 shows the same string or column vibrating in thirds, producing yet another note to

add to the original two. And so the string or column goes on dividing itself into smaller and smaller vibrations, each new division producing yet another harmonic or overtone to add to the others.

Sometimes, with a very long and heavy string, such as the bass string on a guitar, you can actually *see* the several divisions of the string vibrating separately and simultaneously.

This division can in theory go on indefinitely, but in fact the extra notes get weaker and weaker until they have no effect.

It is the shape, size, material and so on of the instrument which determine which of these harmonics shall be produced, and how loudly or softly, and how they shall combine. Each instrument has its own set of harmonics and no two instruments are alike in this respect. Some produce more, some less.

The flute, for instance, has very few overtones and thus produces a very pure

A stretched string vibrates simultaneously as a whole, in halves, in thirds, and so on. Each subdivision has an exact mathematical relationship to all the others

How vibrations from, say, a vibrating string reach the inner ear and are passed on to the brain to give the sensation called 'sound'

or 'cool' sound; a violin has many overtones and it is this which gives the string instruments of the violin family their 'warmth'.

But it is very important that all these harmonics or overtones—thirds, halves, quarters, eighths and so on—should be related to one another.

If they are not, the sound becomes mere noise. An irregular piece of metal, for instance, if beaten with a stick, will give out vibrations of unrelated frequencies—an 'unmusical' sound. However, the same piece of metal, carefully shaped and struck, can give out *related* frequencies and produce a 'musical sound'.

There are three famous orchestral pieces which demonstrate very clearly the different sounds of instruments. *Peter and the Wolf* was written by the great Russian composer Prokofiev in 1936 and has been recorded and played many times. It is a simple fairy story in which

the various characters are represented by different instruments. Peter himself is represented by the strings, the bird by the flute, the duck by the oboe, the cat by the clarinet. Peter's grandfather by the bassoon, the wolf by three French horns, and the hunters by a march theme with lots of percussion.

Saint-Saëns wrote a 'zoological fantasy' in 1858 called *The Carnival of Animals* as a game for his students, which consisted of fourteen brief movements with such names as *Royal Lions March*, *Hens and Cocks*, *The Elephant* and so on, to be played by two pianos and a few other instruments including xylophone and glockenspiel.

Best of all, perhaps, for the purpose of learning to recognize the sounds made by the different instruments, is Benjamin Britten's *The Young Person's Guide to the Orchestra*, written originally for an educational film, *The Instruments of the Orchestra*, in 1946.

4 How Instruments Work

The piano has a string for every note

The flute has one source of basic vibration

Although all instruments work on the principle of producing vibrations to make their varying sounds, the methods of creating the vibrations differ.

Stringed instruments fall into three groups: (i) the bowed, (ii) the plucked, and (iii) the struck. The instruments of the first group (violin, viola, cello and double bass) all are played by drawing a bow across the strings. The bow's horsehair is rubbed with resin, which makes it slightly sticky. As the bow is pulled across the strings it drags them sideways for a tiny fraction of an inch until the natural tension of the string overcomes the pull of the bow and it springs back into position, thus giving rise to the vibration which produces the sound. Instruments of the violin family can also be plucked with the fingers.

The harp, guitar, mandoline and banjo are all played by plucking or sweeping the strings either with the fingers or, in the case of the last three, with a pick or plectrum. The strings of the harpsichord are plucked by quills or leather 'jacks' operated by keys. The strings of the piano are struck by hammers.

The woodwind instruments all contain a column of air which is vibrated by the player's breath impinging on a reed, causing it to vibrate. The vibrating reed imparts its vibration to the column of air in the instrument and thus produces the sound. The clarinet and saxophone have a single reed, the oboe, bassoon and bagpipes a double reed. The exceptions are the flute, wherein the vibration is started not by a reed but by blowing across the lip of a hole in the body of the instrument; and the recorder group of instruments which have a whistle-type mouthpiece.

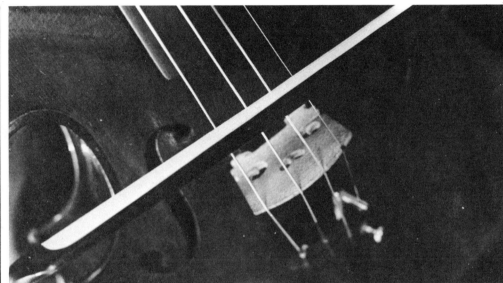

The violin has four strings for all the notes

Brass instruments, whatever their size and shape, all work on an identical principle. The player purses his lips so that they vibrate when air is forced past them, thus causing the column of air in the instrument to vibrate also. The pitch of the note is altered by tightening or slackening the lips and thus increasing or decreasing the speed of the vibrations.

All the various instruments have different ways of producing notes of different pitch. The piano, for instance, does it by having a different string for each note. The same thing occurs with the accordion, mouth organ, pipe organ, vibraphone, xylophone and harpsichord, all of which have a different reed, pipe, bar or key for every note.

The longer the string or pipe, or the larger the metal or wooden bar, the deeper the note. But to understand why the same length string on a violin or guitar produces different pitches, you have to take into account two other factors—the thickness of the strings and the tension they are under. Thicker strings vibrate more slowly and thus produce notes of lower pitch. But all strings, whether thick or thin, have to be tensioned to exactly the right degree in order to produce exactly the right note. You may have seen the string players in an orchestra bowing the open strings with one hand and tightening or slackening the pegs to which the strings are attached with the other. They are simply 'tuning up' before the performance.

It is possible to adjust strings of different thickness so that they produce the same note. But don't try it—the extra strain necessary to get the thicker string to sound the higher note could well snap either the string or its attachments.

In addition to the thickness and tension of the strings there is their length. On all stringed instruments (except the piano, harp and harpsichord) the strings are of virtually the same length. They are shortened by 'stopping'—that is, by the player pressing his fingers on them so that they touch the fingerboard, thus making a new joining point and having the effect of shortening the string. A scale is played on a stringed instrument by moving the 'stopping' fingers along the string from one one end to the other. It would be possible in theory to have just one string (and there is in fact an instrument called a 'one-string fiddle') and to play all the notes on that, but it would be impossible to play fast passages with big jumps between the notes, so the violin player plays part of the scale on one string and then shifts to another string to play the rest. Guitar, banjo and mandoline players also do this if they are playing simple tunes, but because the fingerboard of these instruments is flat they can also play chords (several notes at once) by pressing down ('stopping') several strings at different points all at the same time.

The method of producing different notes on a wind instrument is exactly the same, except that it is the column of air which is lengthened or shortened.

This is done in one of two different ways. In the woodwind instruments (flute, clarinet, oboe, bassoon, saxophone, recorder and so on) the column is made shorter by opening holes in the tube. In some instruments (clarinet, flute, oboe, bassoon, saxophone) the holes are covered by round flat keys operated by levers, either because they are too far apart to be comfortably covered by the fingers, or because of convenience in playing extra notes, or because the acoustically necessary positions of the holes would be awkward for the fingers to cover. In other instruments (fife, recorder) the holes are simply covered by the fingers when a 'long' column of air is wanted. When all the holes or keys are closed the column of air is as long as the tube of the instrument itself, whether this is straight or curved. Generally speaking the moment a hole is uncovered, the column of air changes its length to the distance from the blowing end to where the hole is. There are some exceptions to this, but they do not alter the principle.

A recorder or fife, with few keys or none at all, is therefore simpler to play than a modern flute, clarinet, saxophone or oboe, all of which have a large number of keys. But whether there are keys or holes, the purpose is the same—to change momentarily the length of the column of air inside the instrument.

The brass instruments (trumpet, cornet, French horn, trombone and so on) work on exactly the same principle—lengthening and shortening the column of air inside the tube—but they do it in a different way. Whereas the woodwind instruments do it by closing holes in the body of the instrument, brass instruments do it by adding *extra lengths of tubing*.

If you look at the valves of a brass instrument, you will see that they are surrounded by short pieces of tubing leading into and out of the valves. When a valve is depressed it shunts the air stream through the extra bit of tubing, thus lengthening the overall column of air. The valve is a very complicated piece of mechanism, and each one adds a different length of tubing. Used either singly or in combination they can lengthen the basic tubing six different ways, thus bridging the gaps between the 'open' notes which the player gets by tightening or slackening his lips. The trombone works on the same principle, except that the tubing is lengthened and shortened by moving the slide in and out.

The percussion instruments divide into three classes: those of indeterminate pitch (no definite note) such as the snare drum, bass drum and triangle; those with fixed tuning such as vibraphone, xylophone and bells; and those of variable tuning, the timpani. The pitch of the fixed-tuning instruments is determined by the size of the metal or wood bar or tube, that of timpani partly by size and partly by the degree of tension put upon the head.

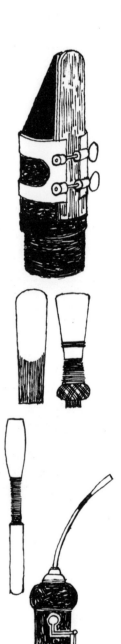

Clarinet mouthpiece (*top*), cor anglais crook and reed (*bottom*), and reeds for saxophone, bassoon and oboe

'La Barre and Other Musicians' by Tournier, showing (*left*) a baryton with 'sympathetic' strings which are not played upon but vibrate in 'sympathetic resonance' with the other strings, and (back and right) wooden keyless flutes

5 The Violin

Yehudi Menuhin

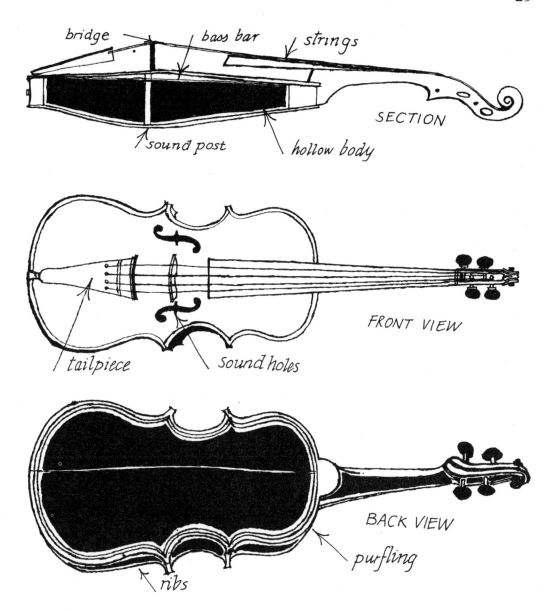

bridge   bass bar   strings

SECTION

sound post   hollow body

tailpiece   sound holes

FRONT VIEW

BACK VIEW

purfling

ribs

The parts of the violin

The violin leads the symphony orchestra and the string quartet. A vast number of solo works have been written for it and it shares with the piano the honour of having given rise to some of the greatest instrumental virtuosi.

It is equally valuable as a solo or as an orchestral instrument. Dance bands have featured its singing tone and there have been great jazz violinists such as Joe Venuti and Stephane Grapelli.

Because of the violin's range and flexibility it is difficult to become an outstanding player.

No one man invented the violin. It is the result of a very long line of developments going back hundreds of years to Near Eastern bowed instruments. The violin first appeared in a more primitive form in the sixteenth century. It was brought to perfection in the eighteenth century by the great Italian masters—Stradivarius, Guarnerius, Amati—and their instruments have never been surpassed. Today the price of one of their violins can range up to £80,000 or more.

The violin is made from about 85 separate pieces of various kinds of wood

Playing position for the violin

Stradivarius violin
—front

—maple, ebony, pine and sycamore among them—glued together and varnished. The selection of the wood, its shaping and its varnishing are the 'secrets' that produce the warm, mellow but powerful tone. There are many modern craftsman-made violins of fine tone, but the master quality of the old ones has never been equalled. There are also fakes, some containing imitation labels of the great makers. Beware of the old violin that has been knocking about the family for years, bearing a 'Stradivarius' label. It is almost certainly not genuine.

The length of a violin is determined by the average length of the human arm from the shoulder to the palm of the hand—about 24 inches. Smaller sizes, which can be three-quarters, half or even smaller, are specially made for children. The strings are made from sheep gut, pig gut, steel or nylon, or from one of these wound with silver or aluminium wire. Inside the body of the instrument, just below the bridge, is the sound post, which has a great deal to do not only with the tone of the instrument but also with its strength. There is a 96-pound pull on the strings and valuable old violins, made in the days when the pitch was lower, have had their necks lengthened and strengthened to take the added strain imposed by the necessity of tighter stringing.

The bow is tremendously important. Consisting of a stick strung end to end with horsehair, at one time it was curved outwards. Today, because of increased

Stradivarius violin
—back

tension, it is curved inwards. At the 'frog' or 'nut' end (the part nearest the hand) there is a screw which is used to tension the hair and which is loosened when the bow is not in use. Resin is rubbed on the hair to make it 'bite' the strings.

The violin is held under the chin on the left shoulder, with the left hand moving freely along the neck of the instrument. Very occasionally a left-handed violinist is encountered—Charlie Chaplin is one—for whom the strings and bridge have to be reversed.

An essential quality for a good violinist is an accurate ear for pitch; the violinist has no keys or frets to guide him as to where he should put his fingers. He has to find his own notes, partly by training but partly by ear. The rocking of the left hand back and forth gives the vibrato which is so essential a part of violin playing, not only in producing its full, rich tone, but in allowing for fine adjustments of pitch.

The violin is capable of a wide range of effects in addition to its normal single-note playing with the bow. Double-stopping (playing two notes at the same time), pizzicato (plucking the strings with the fingers), opened-out chords (arpeggios) across the strings, harmonics (soft and fluty sounds produced by touching the strings lightly, rather than pressing them down firmly) are all effects widely used.

All the orchestral repertory features the violin prominently and the violins (divided into 'first' and 'second' groups) make up nearly half of the normal symphony orchestra. The first violins, whose section leader is leader or concert-master of the whole orchestra, generally have the top line of the melody. The leader is often called upon as a soloist. In *Scheherazade* for instance, the violin represents the beautiful princess telling her stories, whilst in *Peter and the Wolf* it represents Peter. A string quartet always includes two violins as first and second instrument.

If you intend to learn the violin it is a good thing to start early. Some people actually suggest that you should start at four! The reason is that certain muscles are required to be used in ways that are not normal, so the younger you start, the better. However, do not feel that it is impossible to start at a later age. Many people have only started the violin after they were grown up and have had great pleasure from it.

There have been many child virtuosi of the violin—you have probably listened to Yehudi Menuhin and Isaac Stern, who were not only child prodigies, but have gone forward to become adult masters of the violin—and Mozart was another child virtuoso. But perhaps the greatest violinist of them all was Paganini whose playing seemed almost supernaturally brilliant. Not many people are as gifted as these, but even if you never attain such heights, you will find that the violin is an enormously rewarding instrument to take up, with its repertoire ranging from the concerto and the symphony to gipsy melodies such as those arranged by Brahms and Tchaikovsky, and even to imitations of natural sounds such as birdsong and the buzzing of bees!

The magic of this beautiful instrument, in the hands of a master player, covers an infinite range of emotion, almost to the human voice. At this level it becomes almost part of the player's own body, responding through its vibration and the bow to his innermost thoughts and feelings.

6 The Viola

Viola and violin (*right*) compared for size

Much of what has been said in the preceding chapter about the violin applies to the viola—its construction, its range and flexibility, the way it is held and so on. Indeed, to the inexperienced eye there seems to be very little difference between the two instruments.

But the viola is larger and heavier, its range goes down lower by five notes, and its tone is deeper and more sonorous than that of the violin.

The viola is made in three-quarter size, but as there is some variation in size between one maker and another young beginners should search for one which is slightly smaller than average. In any case it is an instrument for the long-armed.

The viola can do anything the violin can do in the way of rapid passages, despite the fact that the distance between notes is fractionally longer. Its tone, however, is not as brilliant as that of the violin.

For a very long time the viola did little more than 'double' the part written for the cello. It was not until the eighteenth century that composers like Gluck, Haydn and Mozart saw its possibilities and gave it individual status among the string section.

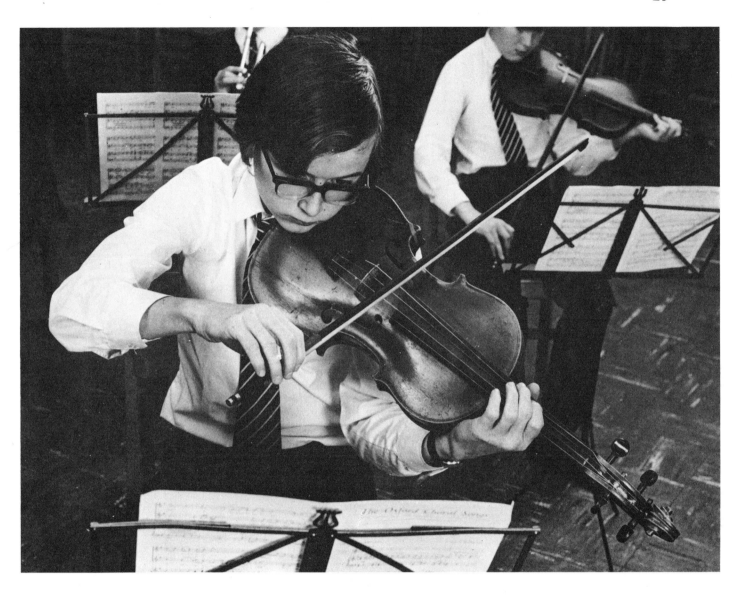

Playing position for
the viola

At one time in its early history the viola was used by violinists when they wanted an instrument with a slightly deeper range. For convenience they wished it to be as much like a violin in size as possible, and violas were made with bodies 15 inches long compared to the modern instrument's 16–17 inches. There was at one time a super instrument with a 19-inch body, but this was a bit of a freak and has long since disappeared. Another long-gone oddity was a viola with a fifth string tuned in unison with the top string of the violin.

The viola plays a tremendously im-portant part in the symphony orchestra and an even more important role in the string quartet (which consists of two violins, viola and cello). Very occasion-ally it is heard in the dance orchestra and in the pop group. It was seldom used as a solo instrument before the end of the last century.

Lionel Tertis and William Primrose, both British, are two of the great viola soloists who have done much to raise the instrument's musical status.

The cost of a viola is as uncertain as that of a violin. It is used less widely than the latter, so far fewer are produced,

which makes the instrument relatively more expensive although its manufacture is no more complicated.

A few great violin makers also made violas and there are quite a number of Stradivarius instruments in existence. Their cost is determined by their rarity as well as by their quality.

The viola is of about the same difficulty as the violin and in the same way compositions for it range from the simple to the extremely difficult.

Whether it is the best instrument for a young player to choose depends in some degree on what opportunities are available for playing it in an ensemble. If there is a need for violas in the school orchestra then the young player will find great satisfaction in learning the instrument. It is unusual and has a beautiful tone. But there is less solo work for the viola and its larger size makes it difficult to handle for anyone much younger than twelve or thirteen.

Many viola players have transferred to the viola from the violin or cello— either because they could not get on with those instruments, or because they preferred the sound of the viola, or because

there was less competition for viola parts and therefore more vacancies for players. It is a thought worth keeping in mind, since most violin techniques can be adapted without much difficulty to the viola. Indeed, the two great viola players mentioned above both started as violinists, transferring to the viola after many years with the violin.

Mozart was very fond of the instrument and played it himself in later years. He wrote interesting parts for it in his string quartets and quintets, adding a second viola for the latter.

There is a viola *Lament* by Richard Rodney Bennett in the film *Lady Caroline Lamb*.

Some other works for viola, most or all of which can be heard on records, are the concertos of Bartók, Walton, Mozart (especially the latter's *Sinfonia Concertante* for violin and viola). In Strauss' *Don Quixote* the viola represents the Don's servant, Sancho Panza. Hindemith (himself a very good viola player) wrote several fine sonatas. Berlioz gives the viola the solo voice in his tone poem *Harold in Italy*.

Above left Lionel Tertis, viola virtuoso

Above The viola in the Ladies' Orchestra, by du Maurier (1875)

7 The Cello

The cello is a member of the violin family, although it is not built to exactly the same proportions. Its full name is 'violoncello'—note the second 'o', not an 'i'—which means 'little bass viol'. But this is a misnomer, since it is not a member of the viol family, which has distinct differences from the violin group. Sometimes the contraction is spelt with an apostrophe—'cello—but the tendency today is to drop the apostrophe. The pronunciation, by the way, is *ch*ello.

The instrument is played between the knees—in earlier times it was held by a short thick peg on the floor but now a collapsible spike in the bottom of the instrument raises it to a convenient playing height.

Like the violin, it is made in three-quarter, half and quarter sizes, so that a child can comfortably tackle it from about seven years old. The distances between notes on the fingerboard are, of course, greater than those on the violin and viola, so the player has to develop greater stretch in the fingers.

The cello can do most things that the smaller instruments can do—pizzicato (plucking the strings), arpeggios, double-stopping, harmonics and so on, and has an exceptionally rich and sonorous tone, very suited to both solo and ensemble playing.

Its construction very largely follows that of the smaller members of the violin family, and like them, numbers the great Italian makers among its creators. In 1572 Amati of Cremona in Italy, one of the famous violin makers, made a cello which Pope Pius V gave to King Charles IX, of

Playing position for the cello

Pablo Casals, master cellist, as a young man

Pablo Casals at practice in his hotel bedroom (1945)

France and there are also in existence a few cellos made by Stradivarius.

The bow of the cello is slightly shorter and heavier than the violin bow, but is held in the same manner and is similarly resined to give it 'bite' on the strings.

One special difference between the playing of the violin or viola and the cello is that with the cello the thumb is used in the high positions, partly to 'stop' the string and partly to help the player find the correct position.

In early days the cello had the fairly dull job of playing the bass notes along with the double bass. In string quartets it usually played the bass part, very seldom having a melody to play. But Haydn and Mozart recognized its possibilities and it was given running passages of its own. Finally, Beethoven brought it out fully in his orchestral works,

chamber music and sonatas.

Its most effective place is with the other members of the violin family in symphony orchestras, string quartets and chamber orchestras. It is occasionally met with in the larger semi-dance-semi-light orchestra groups where it provides a solid sonorous voice, both solo and in conjunction with other instruments.

The cello is fairly often heard as an unaccompanied instrument. Bach's *Saraband* from Suite 3 is one of the best-known solo cello works—it is one of six suites for unaccompanied cello, dating back to 1720 and is of extreme difficulty.

As with all the other string instruments a good ear for tuning is essential, there being no frets or keys to guide the player in placing his fingers. Also as with all instruments it is difficult to play at a master level, but at lower levels it can

Jacqueline du Pré,
world-famous cellist,
and her concert pianist
husband, Daniel
Barenboim

Elizabethan viol player

produce very rewarding results quite soon. In particular, its rich tone makes it very suitable for simple solo playing.

For those who contemplate home playing, the cello—either alone or accompanied by piano and one or two violins—is an ideal instrument. It is useful to know, in this context, that like all members of the violin family, the cello can be muted. A wood or metal clip is placed on the bridge and reduces the volume considerably as well as changing the tone to a thin sweetness.

More modern composers have written challenging works for the instrument—Schumann, Dvořák, Elgar and Hindemith among them. Strauss used it to represent the Don in *Don Quixote* (in which the viola represents Sancho Panza).

Listen to the cello in live performances or recordings of Britten's *Cello Symphony* (written for the great Russian cellist, Rostrapovich), the slow movement of Brahms' *Piano Concerto No. 2 in B Flat*, the slow movement of the Shostakovitch *Symphony No. 1*, Tchaikovsky's Pas de Deux in *Swan Lake* Ballet Music, and Saint-Saëns' 'The Swan' in his *Carnival of the Animals*.

The Brazilian composer, Villa-Lobos, wrote several works for massed cellos—in one case for eight cellos and in two cases for eight cellos and a soprano soloist.

8 The Double Bass

The double bass is the foundation and rock on which the entire string section is built. Its steady booming voice is so valuable that it is in demand in many other combinations than the symphony orchestra—the dance band, the modern jazz unit, the military band, even occasionally the pop group, although they tend to prefer its cousin, the bass guitar.

Although a member of the string section, the double bass is related both to the true violin family and to the viols, which differ from the violins in having a flat instead of a curved back and sloping shoulders. Both these characteristics are shared by the double bass. However, the viols also have frets which the double bass does not. It is sometimes referred to as a 'bass viol' which is incorrect.

Other names for it are string bass (to distinguish it from the brass bass—see Chapter 20), the contrabass, or even, in the USA, the 'bull fiddle'.

The double bass rests on a peg. It is a very large instrument and the performer has to stand, or at least perch on a high stool, while playing it. The strings are long and thick and require strong fingers to press them down, but not so strong as to preclude the instrument being played by 13–14-year-olds, boy or girl. There are many girl players of the double bass to be found in school orchestras—so do not be put off by its size.

Perhaps the greatest bass player who ever lived was Bottesini, who took up the instrument almost by accident. Applying for admission to Milan Conservatory in 1832 at the age of eleven, he found there was only one vacancy and that was for a student of the double bass. He didn't hesitate a moment, took the vacancy and embarked on a career that was to make him famous as both a virtuoso player and composer of music for the instrument. Koussevitzky, the great conductor, also started his career as a bass player.

Even though the bass is the largest instrument in the orchestra, there have been experiments in the past to make it even bigger in order to get still lower notes. In the Museum of the Paris Conservatoire there is a gigantic instrument *eleven feet* high, called the octo-bass. The stretch between notes was too big even for the largest hands, and the strings were 'stopped' by means of steel 'fingers' operated by levers.

The bow of the double bass was originally convex shaped and had enough space between the stick and the hair for the player to put his hand between them and hold the bow palm upwards. This style called Dragonetti after a great virtuoso

Playing position for the double bass

Double bass and violin compared for size

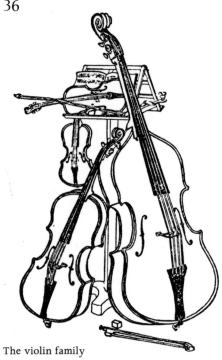

The violin family

The viol family

soloist, was eventually mostly replaced by a short stubby bow that looks and handles like a cello bow.

Despite the size of the instrument there have been many players of such skill that concertos were written for them containing fast passages that would tax the abilities of a cellist. Dragonetti, who was a friend of Beethoven, showed the composer what the instrument could do and in his Fourth, Fifth and Ninth Symphonies Beethoven gave the bass part fast running passages and large leaping lines. Other composers followed —Schubert, Saint-Saëns, Tchaikovsky, Stravinsky and others all wrote passages for the bass which put it in the solo instrument class.

However, the instrument is seldom asked to perform virtuoso feats and is mostly confined to fairly slow bowed or plucked passages well within the abilities of a young player.

At one time the bass had five strings and one can still find a few old instruments of this kind. But nearly all instruments today are four-stringed. Unlike the other members of the string section they are tuned in fourths instead of fifths, the reason being to make the span shorter before moving across to the next string in playing scale passages. The music for the bass is written an octave higher than it sounds, in order to avoid too many extra lines below the stave.

In dance and jazz groups the instrument is played almost entirely pizzicato (plucked by the fingers). Long periods of this can be hard on the fingers and some players wear a leather finger stall. But the finger soon hardens and makes protection unnecessary. Half and three-quarter sizes are available and many models are smaller than the standard, and thus very suitable for young players. Incidentally, the great virtuosi of the past —Dragonetti, Bottesini and the rest—all used rather smaller-than-standard instruments which allowed quicker response of the strings and was easier for the player to manipulate.

Listen to the double bass players (there are quite often eight or ten of them in a symphony orchestra) in Saint-Saëns' 'The Elephant' in *Carnival of the Animals*, in the slow movement of Mahler's *Symphony No. 1*, and in the Introduction to the last movement of Beethoven's *Ninth Symphony*.

9 The Harp

Junior school harp

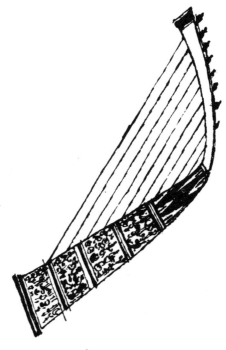

Ancient Egyptian harp

Most instruments have altered considerably since their inception, but none has been modified more than the harp. Possibly the first harp was derived from a hunter's bow. Certainly there are pictures of harps on ancient vases 5,000 years old, and there is in the New York Metropolitan Museum of Art an ancient Egyptian harp at least 2,500 years old. There is also an example in the British Museum.

These early harps were merely a number of strings of various length stretched between a curved upright and a soundbox of some kind—the soundbox was essential to amplify the sound of the instrument, since without it the strings by themselves were almost inaudible even when plucked strongly.

The ancient Greeks and Romans knew and used the harp and to the Welsh and Irish they became national symbols which were used by bards to accompany their heroic songs and stories. An old Welsh saying was that the three necessities for a man's home were a virtuous wife, a cushion for the best chair, and a harp.

But these primitive harps were severely limited in both range and the number of notes they could play. Many attempts were made to overcome these handicaps but always the innovators ran into the same problem—if there was to be a string for every note of the scale, then the range was only an octave or so; if it was to cover two or three octaves, then all the flats and sharps had to be omitted otherwise the 'stretch' was too far for the player's arm to reach. At one time, about the end of the sixteenth century, an attempt was made to solve this problem by having two rows of strings—one for the naturals and one for the sharps and flats. But this was too difficult to play—although Monteverdi actually used such an instrument in his opera *Orfeo*.

A solution was in sight when some Swiss harp makers had the idea of fastening small hooks to the strings which could be *pulled* to make the semitones. But this also failed because it meant the player had only one hand available for most of the performance. Eventually, in 1720, a Bavarian instrument maker hit on the final idea—to operate the hooks by means of pedals depressed by the feet. Then, in 1819, the Alsatian–Frenchman, Érard, patented the double-action harp, whereby the pedals were capable of moving the tightening devices (now discs with pegs in place of hooks) two steps instead of the previous one. With seven pedals this gave the harp a full and wide range.

The strings, which are plucked from both sides, are of different colours so that the player can more easily distinguish one from the other—all strings sounding C are red, all those sounding F are blue or purple and the intermediate ones are not coloured.

Strings can be plucked singly or in groups as chords, the notes being sounded all together or in rapid succession as an arpeggio (the word arpeggio actually means 'played like a harp'). The player uses the thumbs and all the fingers with the exception of the little finger.

Various tones can be produced, depending on where the string is plucked. Near the soundboard it produces a thin guitar-like sound; harmonics are played by very lightly touching the string at the midway point with the palm of the hand while it is being plucked by the fingers.

The harp's most characteristic sound is the glissando, produced by a sweeping motion of the hands.

The harp may be used as a solo instrument, as one of a chamber group, or as a member of the symphony orchestra, and it never fails to attract attention, not only for its delicate sweetness of sound but also for its beautiful appearance.

The compass of the harp is less than that of the piano—$5\frac{1}{2}$ octaves. This range, however, gives it almost unlimited scope for use in the orchestra or as a solo instrument and composers have not been slow to take advantage of it. Mozart wrote a *Concerto* for flute and harp, Debussy produced a Sonata for Flute, Violin and Harp, Berlioz used *two* harps for the first time in his *Symphonie Fantastique* and there are harp parts in almost every modern composition. Wagner used an ensemble of harps to represent the River Rhine in his *Ring* operas.

So far, the harp has not penetrated into more modern musical groups, although there have been one or two players who have specialized in jazz solos. And there was, of course, the 'dumb' member of the Marx Brothers who played some spectacular harp solos in every film they made. It is of some interest, by the way, that Harpo Marx was self-taught and for many years played with the instrument resting on the 'wrong' shoulder.

It is an extremely difficult instrument to play—which makes Harpo's skill with it all the more remarkable—and a very costly one to buy. For this reason it is hardly ever found in junior orchestras unless the orchestra organizer is lucky enough to 'happen to know' some young person so attracted by the instrument's beauty as to have acquired one somehow.

Some folk singers use a small harp to accompany themselves. This is usually what is called a Gaelic harp, not to be confused with the large orchestral double-action harp described above.

Lady harpist—late eighteenth century

10 The Guitar

Playing position for the guitar

The origins of the guitar go back to antiquity. It was known to exist in Northern Africa and may have reached Europe through the influence of the Arabs. In Spain, where it eventually became the national instrument, one of the oldest printed books was a guitar tutor dated 1500. Since then it has spread and developed in many different directions.

The guitar has a flat back, curved sides, a circular sound hole and six strings made of gut, nylon, silk, metal or wire-covered nylon. Frets on the fingerboard ensure the correct position of the fingers. It is played by plucking or (for chords) sweeping the strings with the fingers or with a plectrum, which is a small piece of tortoiseshell, plastic or felt.

The classical, Spanish or 'finger-style' guitar as played by Segovia, John Williams, Julian Bream and others, is the most simply constructed of all the various forms of the instrument, but its quality can range enormously from the cheapest of factory-made versions to instruments, perfectly fashioned and decorated with elaborate inlay. The classical guitar is usually slightly smaller than the other forms, to give it finer tone and greater dynamic range—that is, variations in loudness and softness. All the six strings of a classical guitar are of gut. Even the great Stradivarius turned his supreme skill to guitar making and produced instruments of really superb quality.

Many of the great composers have written for the guitar—Boccherini, de Falla, Weber, Berlioz and Britten amongst them. The great violinist, Paganini, devoted three years to mastering the instrument and subsequently composed most of his violin music on the guitar.

The 'folk' guitar—that is the instrument used by many singers of today to accompany themselves—is very like the classical version, except that it is usually larger, not so costly and often has a tortoiseshell or plastic shield added to protect the body from damage by the plectrum striking it. It is played either in single notes or in chords, all four fingers and even the thumb being used to 'stop' the strings. A metal device known as a *capo* is often used to simplify playing. It is clipped on to the fingerboard, thus effectively shortening the strings, and is used to save the player the trouble of learning extra chord shapes for different keys. Played in this way the guitar is perhaps the simplest of all instruments, and it is possible to learn to play basic chords after only a few hours' tuition.

The guitar used in the pop group is a very different instrument, although it has the fretted fingerboard, flat bridge and six strings common to the other forms. The difference lies in the fact that for its resonance and tone it depends on magnetic pickups and electrical amplification, plus the addition of various levers and knobs to control volume and produce special effects far removed from those

of the standard guitar. It is available in both 'acoustic' and 'semi-acoustic' form —that is with a hollow or a partly hollow body—or 'solid' which, as its name implies, has a shallow, totally solid body. All forms are equipped with two metal strings at the bottom and four gut for the remainder. This is the 'rhythm' or 'lead' guitar of the pop group. It is played with a plectrum or pick and usually uses a capo.

Amplification is its main feature. Whereas the classical guitar would not be heard against all the other instruments, a single electric guitar with its attendant amplifiers and powerful loudspeakers is capable of drowning an entire brass band. Its cost can be considerable, for the modern electric guitar is useless without all its attendant amplifying gear.

First cousin to the above is the bass guitar, which is similar in every respect

Early eighteenth-century triple-strung French guitars

Andrés Segovia, virtuoso Spanish guitarist

The Slade pop group
with electric guitars

Modern Spanish or
'acoustic' guitar

except that it has four strings (or, very occasionally, six) all of which are heavier and thicker in order to produce a deeper range. It replaces the double bass in pop groups and is beginning to do so in other recording and broadcasting groups. Single notes are played with a plectrum.

Then there are 'jumbo' guitars, the same as the classical version but with a larger body, usually 16 inches wide by $4\frac{1}{2}$ inches deep compared with the more standard $14\frac{1}{2}$ inches by $4\frac{1}{2}$ inches. The added size increases resonance and volume. Some of these extra-large guitars are equipped with twelve strings, the top two being tuned in unison and the remainder in octaves. The purpose again is to give still greater resonance and volume. There is even a two-necked guitar, one neck carrying the normal acoustic guitar's six strings, the other equipped with the 'folk' twelve strings.

A 'dobro' guitar is standard acoustic size, but has a hollowed-out metal back and six metal strings. It has a twangy sound and is used in 'soul' or 'gospel' type playing.

Another cousin, a little further re-moved, is the Hawaiian guitar. This began life as the ordinary Spanish guitar, but was played with a 'steel'—a flat metal bar—to stop the strings instead of the fingers. Sliding this steel from one posi-tion to the other produces the instru-ment's characteristic wailing sound. The guitar is played laid flat across the performer's lap. Today the Hawaiian guitar, or 'steel' guitar, has in some cases followed the lead of its pop group relative and abandoned its body in exchange for electric amplification with loudspeakers. It is still played with the sliding steel bar, however, and produces much the same effect as the older version.

The recordings of Segovia, Williams and Bream will all provide magnificent examples of the classical guitar; old timers Eddie Lang and Django Reinhardt splen-didly represent jazz of the 1930s and all of today's pop groups use 'rhythm' guitars and bass guitars. Singers such as Joan Baez demonstrate the use of the 'folk' guitar as accompaniment. The volume of guitar music is great, ranging from the simplest of folk song arrange-ments to really intricate and difficult classical works.

11 The Banjo, Mandoline, Ukulele and Sitar

None of these instruments can properly be described as an 'orchestral' instrument, but they *are* musical instruments played by lots of people and with musical organizations devoted to them. Therefore they do have a proper place in this book.

They are all cousins of the guitar, inasmuch as they are all plucked with the fingers or a plectrum, they all have flat bridges (important in that they cannot therefore, be played with a bow), they all have fretted necks (that is, the fingerboards have transverse inserts to indicate where the fingers are placed to produce the desired notes. Apart from these important similarities, however, they have widely different backgrounds.

The banjo derives from a native African

The banjo began life on the plantations of the southern states of America

The 5-string G banjo

The mandoline with four pairs of strings

instrument called a banjar, made from an animal skin stretched over a hollow gourd, with a wooden neck to support the strings. It was supposed to have been brought to America by the African slaves, by whom it was used to accompany plantation dances and songs. Over the years it developed into a circular hollow body made of metal or wood, with a tensioned drum skin, tightening screws, fretted neck and five or six metal strings.

It is played either by strumming chords or playing single-string melody or a mixture of both. It became the favoured instrument of the minstrel shows of early 1900s and was adopted by the first ragtime bands of the 1910 period. In early jazz it reigned unchallenged until the coming of the more sophisticated guitar. It still has many faithful adherents and the Big Ben Banjo Band is still today a steady best seller on gramophone records.

The mandoline, which possesses the basic features outlined above, has a very different background. It is a member of the lute family and has that instrument's characteristic body like a pear cut in half lengthwise. Its other special characteristic is that it has *pairs* of strings tuned exactly

alike, the four pairs being tuned like the violin. The method of playing is unlike that of any other instrument. Using a plectrum, the player strums back and forth rapidly on a pair of strings to produce the instrument's characteristic tinkling, tremolo sound.

Its home background is Southern Italy, where it is used to accompany folk songs and love songs, but it has not gone unnoticed by the great composers. Beethoven wrote several short pieces for it, Mozart used it in *Don Giovanni* as a seranading instrument, and Mahler (who never overlooked any instrument) used it in his *Sixth Symphony*.

It has a curiously individual sound which always evokes the idea of Neapolitan serenading in the Mediterranean moonlight. It is also fairly easy to play, but apart from self-accompaniment it is not widely used.

The ukulele just escapes the category of 'toy instrument'. A small four-string guitar emanating from Portugal, it became the favourite string instrument of the Hawaiians, whence it emigrated to the United States in the 1920s as an easy-to-play instrument for self-accompaniment at parties, picnics, college singsongs and the like. Occasionally it reached the professional stage and Cliff Edwards ('Ukulele Ike') in the States and George Formby in England made it an integral part of their acts. It became so widely used that nearly all popular sheet music included what is called 'tablature' (small diagrams of the fingerboards showing where the fingers should be placed to produce the required chords). Although still to be found in the Hawaiian Islands, it has virtually been replaced elsewhere by the guitar, which has an altogether more powerful and pleasant tone.

Lovers of the sitar will hardly be pleased to find this noble instrument included in a chapter containing such humble relations as the ukulele and, indeed, they are literally worlds apart, both in origin, sound, complexity and extreme difficulty in performance.

Springing from the Persian lute and the Indian vina, the sitar is tuned to a scale totally unlike anything in the Western world. Its technique is profoundly difficult and mastery of it comes only with a lifetime of practice.

It is usually equipped with seven strings which are fingered, plus anything up to eighteen 'drone' strings which sound in sympathy and add resonance. The curved metal frets standing above the fingerboard are movable and are adjusted before playing to produce the required tonality. It is plucked by a metal thumb pick, and pitch may be altered *after* the string has been plucked by pulling the strings sideways across the frets to produce the delicate shadings of tone which are characteristic of the instrument.

Attempts have been to introduce the sitar into pop groups, but with little success, its difficult technique defeating all but the most accomplished guitarists. The Beatles, in particular, showed great interest in it.

Other instruments of the plucked-strings group which should be mentioned are the bouzouki, the traditional Greek instrument like a mandoline with an elongated neck, four pairs of strings tuned one note lower than the first four strings of the guitar; and the Russian balalaika, again somewhat like a mandoline, but triangular, with either three or six strings.

The 4-string tenor banjo as played in the Temperance Seven

12 The Flute and Piccolo

As has been said earlier, the flute is one of the very earliest instruments, descending directly from the hollowed-out bone whistle of Stone Age man.

At what stage in history, and for what reason, the idea occurred of blowing across a hole in the *side* of the tube instead of blowing across the *end*, nobody knows, except that it originated in the East.

The flute is the soprano voice of the woodwind section and both it and its smaller brother the piccolo are the only two orchestral woodwind instruments to be played without a reed. The player's

Sir Geraint Evans in Mozart's 'The Magic Flute'

Playing position of the piccolo

Playing position of the flute

breath, striking the opposite edge of the hole, sets in motion the column of air inside the instrument and thus produces the sound.

Despite its classification as *wood*wind, it is today mostly made in metal—nickel-silver alloy, silver, gold or even in platinum (which incidentally produces a quite 'dead' sound!). It was in the early nineteenth century that Theodore Boehm, a Munich jeweller, engineer and flautist (somebody who plays the flute is called a flautist, not a flutist!), evolved a method of keys, plates and levers which for the first time enabled the holes in the instrument to be made of the right sizes and in the acoustically correct places. This system was so successful that it remains basically unaltered to this day and has been adopted by other woodwind instruments. Today, what is known as the 'closed G sharp' is the standard modification for flutes and piccolos.

Flutes have been used in orchestras ever since the 1600s, when composers had their choice of the vertical recorder-type flute and the transverse, or cross, flute. But by the latter half of the eighteenth century the transverse flute—the one we know today—had completely taken over. Haydn and Mozart wrote concertos for the flute, and Gluck's *Dance of the Blessed Spirits*; Rossini's *William Tell*, Ravel's *Daphnis and Chloe* and Debussy's *Après-Midi d'un Faune* and *Syrinx*, the latter based on the legend mentioned in Chapter 1, all show it off to fine advantage. The flute represents the Bird in *Peter and the Wolf*.

The piccolo is identical to the flute except that it is half its size and is pitched an octave higher. It goes higher than any other orchestral instrument and has a shrill, penetrating sound that stands out even above the loudest passages of the orchestra. The fife, found in military bands particularly, resembles the piccolo, but has no keys.

Beethoven used the piccolo in the last movements of his Fifth and Ninth Symphonies, Berlioz in his *Symphonie Fantastique* and Tchaikovsky in his *Nutcracker Suite*. One of the best-known piccolo passages is in Sousa's *Stars and Stripes Forever* march.

There is also an alto flute (frequently miscalled a bass flute), four notes lower than the standard flute, and a true bass flute, often called a contrabass flute to avoid confusion with the alto flute. But

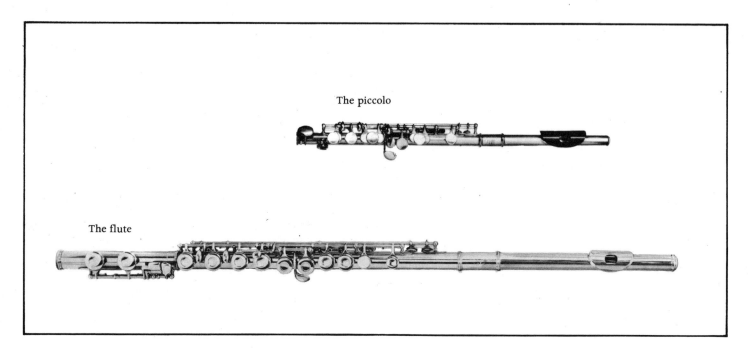

The piccolo

The flute

both these instruments are met with very rarely except in some of the more venturesome modern orchestrations. The alto flute can be heard in Ravel's *Daphnis and Chloe* and Stravinsky's *Rite of Spring*.

Playing the ordinary flute and piccolo is not too difficult except in fast passages (which are often written for the piccolo) and is well within the capabilities of any youngster from the age of ten or eleven. Good even teeth are a necessity, since it would be difficult to make a good 'embouchure' (that is, the pursing of the lips) if the upper or lower teeth were much out of line with their opposites.

It is not often realized that the flute does not call for much breath—surprisingly, the smaller piccolo calls for more pressure. Both instruments call for considerable breath control and the piccolo is usually taken up only after some ability has been achieved on the flute.

An oddity which is worth mentioning but is never met with in orchestras, is the nose flute, found in Hawaii and adjacent islands. It is played by blowing down one nostril, the other being plugged with a finger or piece of cloth. It has few holes but in the hands of an expert can skip about very busily.

The use of the ordinary flute is not confined to the symphony orchestra. It is found in small chamber groups, in military bands and quite often in the more advanced jazz and pop groups, where it is fast growing in favour.

One of the useful aspects of the flute is that it is a non-transposing instrument —that is, it sounds as written, unlike woodwind instruments such as the clarinet, which do not. The value of this is apparent more in home playing than in orchestral playing because the performer can play straight from the piano copy or violin part without any problems of transposing.

For some reason, the flute has always been very popular with royalty. Frederick II, King of Prussia, not only played it but composed many works for it; Stanislas, King of Poland, was also a player and had his portrait painted with his favourite instrument.

The largest variety and ensemble of flutes can be heard in the Northern Ireland Flute Bands, which are as popular there as brass bands are in England.

13 The Clarinet

Playing position for the clarinet

Left-hand position—note keys operated by side of the forefinger and by the little finger

The clarinet is probably the most popular and most widely used of all the woodwind instruments. It is equally at home in the symphony orchestra, the military band, the dance band, way-out jazz units, and pop groups. Its range is very wide; it can go from very soft to very loud and back again immediately; it can purr in its bottom register and shriek at its top.

Its ancestry goes back to the mediaeval single-reed chalumeau which was used until the end of the eighteenth century, when Johann Denner, an instrument maker of Nuremberg, evolved a very much improved version, which he called a clarinet because its upper register resembled that of a high-pitched trumpet, the Italian name of which was the clarino.

Today, it is made of blackwood or

Benny Goodman

The clarinet 'embouchure'—front

The clarinet 'embouchure'—side

ebonite, with a complicated system of 17 keys and six rings, based on the Boehm system (see flute). Like the flute, the clarinet has a cylindrical bore—that is, has the same internal diameter throughout its entire length except for the bell—which has an important effect on the tone and the production of the higher notes.

There is a whole family of clarinets and it is as well to understand which is which, especially if one is contemplating buying a second-hand one. At the top of the range, and most used in the military band, is the small E-flat instrument. Next comes the B-flat—by far the most used and undoubtedly the one the learner will want; next comes the A-natural—this is used only in the symphony orchestra for playing in the more difficult 'sharp' keys; then comes the E-flat alto (not to be confused with the *small* E-flat, which is exactly half its length); and finally the B-flat bass. There are others but they are so rarely used as to make it unnecessary to list them here. The B-flat is the 'standard' instrument, with the B-flat bass being used occasionally in large orchestras when a specially deep rich sound is required.

The various letters used in the descriptions above (E-flat, B-flat, etc.) indicate the instrument's 'natural key'—that is, its simplest fingering and also to indicate its size. The purpose of having instruments built in these special keys is to reduce the difficulty of reading and fingering music with lots of sharps or flats. They are called 'transposing' instruments. This need not bother the beginner, since the music is always written in the easiest keys for the instrument, and the fingering is the same on all the instru-

ments, whatever key they are built in. A small handicap, however, is that the player cannot read directly off music written for a non-transposing instrument such as the piano or violin without mentally transposing—that is, playing a note other than the one which is written. This may sound terribly complicated but it comes easily with practice and professional musicians do it as a matter of course.

The clarinet is played with a single reed —a flat piece of cane specially shaped and scraped to wafer thinness at one end. This is fastened to a mouthpiece, which is wedge shaped and open underneath, and held tightly over the open end of the instrument by an adjustable metal clip called a ligature. The usual system of playing is with the tip of the mouthpiece (and the tip of the reed) placed in the mouth, resting on the lower lip, with the upper teeth resting on the upper side of the mouthpiece. The breath of the player causes the tip of the reed to vibrate and thus put in motion the column of air in the instrument.

Second-hand instruments can of course be bought, but here expert advice is needed. Apart from the danger of getting stuck with an out-of-date model, there is the risk of cracks, shaky keywork and worn 'pads' (the leather or nylon discs which cover the holes). The cost of having an old instrument in poor condition repadded and re-sprung can be considerable. Buy either from a reputable dealer or, if buying privately, use the services of a knowledgeable friend.

Music for the clarinet is almost endless. The instrument is used in thousands of symphonic works, to say nothing of records by jazz groups. Some famous compositions which use the clarinet as a soloist (all of them can be found in the record libraries), are: Rimsky-Korsakov's *Capriccio Espagnol*, Sibelius' *Symphony No. 1*, Mozart's *Clarinet Concerto* (versions of which are available from many famous clarinet players including one by the jazz king, Benny Goodman), and the Brahms' *Quintet*. It represents the Cat in *Peter and the Wolf* and the Cuckoo in *Carnival of the Animals*. The bass clarinet can be heard to great effect in Tchaikovsky's *Dance of the Sugarplum Fairy* in his *Nutcracker Suite*. Records of the Original Dixieland Jazz Band, which made the first-ever jazz records, featured the clarinet and more recent masters such as Benny Goodman, Woody Hermann and others brought jazz clarinet playing to an astonishing level of virtuosity.

The B flat clarinet

The B flat bass clarinet

Elizabethan player of the bombard—a member of the oboe family

Old three-key clarinet

14 The Oboe and Cor Anglais

When next you go to a concert you may be surprised to see a few of the musicians, during the preliminary tuning-up period, apparently holding unlit cigarettes between their lips. In fact it is not a cigarette but a reed, and the musicians are oboe players moistening the reed of their delicate instrument before playing —essential if they are to get the thin sweet tone so characteristic of the instrument.

The reed is a piece of cane folded double, then cut into two and bound on to a short metal tube, the unbound double end being then shaved and thinned with special tools. The reed is held between

Playing position for
the oboe

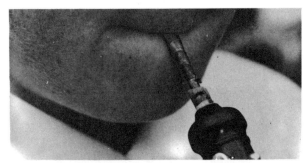

The oboe 'embouchure'
Position of the hands on the oboe

the lips, not touching the teeth, and the pressure the player exerts with his lips on the reed controls the tone and the pitch. It is quite a difficult trick to learn to do well.

The oboe is not an easy instrument to play. It has fifteen or more keys and plates and levers to be manipulated, but this is no more complicated than the flute or clarinet. It is the control of the breath which is difficult—the tiny aperture between the two ends of the reeds will close up altogether if too much breath is directed at them, and the player has to 'hold back' rather than blow hard. The oboe needs less air than any other wind instrument. Long passages can be played without taking extra breath, merely by holding air in the lungs and exhaling gently. The technique of playing the oboe has been compared with swimming under water!

All instruments have a long history, and the oboe's is not only longer than most but also more clearly defined. The Greeks played an instrument called the aulos—which had double reeds very similar to those of the oboe family. But there the likeness ends because the aulos player had to blow with such strength that it was customary to bind his cheeks with leather in case they burst!

It was not until the 1650s, when a certain Jean Hotteterre, who played the bagpipes in the orchestra of the French Court, attempted to improve the mediaeval shawm by reshaping its body (it is now conical—i.e. narrow at the top end and wider at the bell end), adding extra finger holes and redesigning its mouthpiece, that the modern oboe came into existence to become an almost instant success with the composers of the period. Its name comes from the French *hautbois* —literally 'high wood', and the modern instrument is usually made of rosewood but occasionally of ebonite.

Many great composers have delighted in writing for the oboe. Handel wrote concertos for it, and so did Albinoni,

Mozart and Vaughan Williams. It is heard to great effect in the second movement of Schubert's *C Major Symphony* and in the second movement of Tchaikovsky's *Fourth Symphony* and Berlioz' *Benvenuto Cellini Overture*. It represents the Duck in *Peter and the Wolf*.

One of the unusual duties of the oboe is to sound the 'A' to which the whole orchestra tunes. The reason for this is not that there is no latitude in tuning the oboe but because of its pure and penetrating sound.

First cousin to the oboe is the cor anglais (sometimes but not often called the English horn, though it is neither English in origin nor a horn). It is half an octave lower than the oboe, has a very rich sonorous tone and a noticeably different tone colour—owing, at least in part, to its bulbous bell and long curved metal mouthpiece stem.

The cor anglais is sometimes a permanent member of the oboe section, sometimes merely 'doubled' by one of the oboists for a particular solo passage. Its fingering is identical with that of the oboe but because of the longer spaces between holes these are all covered with plates, unlike the holes in the oboe, many of which are covered only by the fingers. The cor anglais reed is slightly larger and, because of the added weight, the instrument is supported by a cord round the player's neck. It is a transposing instrument, sounding a note a fifth lower than the written note. (The problem of transposing is explained more fully in the previous chapter.)

There are other members of the oboe family—the oboe d'amore (pitched between the oboe and the cor anglais), a favourite instrument of J. S. Bach; the heckelphone, a kind of baritone oboe used by Strauss and Delius; and an oddity called the sarrusophone, a wind band instrument made of brass which was originally intended to rival the saxophone and is described in Chapter 16.

The cor anglais

A scene from Prokofief's 'Peter and the Wolf' in which the oboe represents The Duck

15 The Bassoon

Although the bassoon is a member of the oboe family, it rates a chapter to itself because it is such an important instrument in the orchestra and because there is such a need for bassoon players.

It is the bass not only of the oboe family but of all the woodwinds, and yet its upper notes are quite high, giving it altogether a very wide range of over three octaves. This means a considerable variation in tone quality, from a deep resonant bass to a pure and penetrating extreme top register. Because of this fact, plus the ability of the instrument to 'move' very quickly and skip about easily, it has been called the 'clown of the orchestra'. There is little justification for this old joke which is certainly not one that appeals to lovers of the instrument.

It has a length of over eight feet but is doubled back on to itself into a U shape to enable the player to reach all the seven-teen to twenty-two keys, and is usually made of maple. It is quite heavy and is supported by a sling round the player's neck. School models are made with extra touch plates so that the distances between the holes can be easily spanned. Like all the oboe family it has a conical-shaped interior (i.e. narrower at the mouthpiece and widening towards the 'bell') and a double reed (much bigger than the oboe reed—about $\frac{1}{2}$ inch across). Also like the oboe, it can be tuned only by moving the reed on the mouthpiece crook, and there is very little latitude. Sometimes a second crook is used to help with tuning problems. It is not a transposing instrument.

It is an unusual-looking instrument—like a log of wood with a straw (the mouthpiece crook) sticking out of it. The Italians and Germans think it looks like a bundle of sticks and call it the *fagotto* and *Fagott* respectively, which means

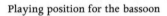
Playing position for the bassoon

The instrument is carried on a cord sling (seen just in front of the player's tie)

Crook and 'embouchure' of the bassoon

Position of the hands on the bassoon—note long 'tracker rods' to operate distant keys

just that in their languages.

There are two different methods of keywork—called the French or Buffet and the German or Heckel systems, of which the latter is the more favoured. You can usually tell which the instrument is by a white ivory ring at the top of the bell in the German system.

Because of its weight it is usually considered not to be suitable for anyone below the age of, say, twelve, although determination to play this fascinating instrument can often overcome the age limitation. The instrument takes to pieces (4) and can be packed away very conveniently in a carrying case. Muting of a rather rough and ready kind can be accomplished by stuffing a handkerchief into the bell.

Ready-made reeds can be bought but many professional players prefer to make their own to suit their particular requirements.

There are not as many solo works for the bassoon as for some other instruments; Vivaldi wrote half a dozen concertos and

Mozart wrote one which has become famous during this century through the celebrated bassoonist Archie Camden. Many composers use the instrument extensively in their works. Lully began this trend in 1674 when he used the bassoon with two oboes to make a trio in his operas. *The Sorcerer's Apprentice* by Paul Dukas, brought to wider fame by the Walt Disney film *Fantasia* of some years ago, uses the bassoon to great effect. Tchaikovsky used it to play a gentle melody in his *Fifth Symphony* and to express tragic feelings in his *Sixth Symphony*. The opening of Stravinsky's *Rite of Spring* and of Bartók's *Dance Suite* are other examples worth listening to. The bassoon represents the Grandfather in *Peter and the Wolf*.

The bassoon has a big brother—a very big brother—called the contrabassoon, or double bassoon. This is a huge instrument with a tube length of over eighteen feet. This enormous length is folded into *four*, finishing up with a brass bell usually pointing *downwards*. The instrument is

Nineteenth-century bassoon player from the Degas painting 'Les Musiciens à l'Orchestre' in the Louvre. Note the simpler keywork

Below
The contrabassoon. It is played resting on the ground owing to its considerable weight. The curved pipe at top right is the mouthpiece crook

too heavy even to be carried on a sling round the player's neck and rests on the ground supported by a stout metal spike. Some contrabassoons have been made entirely of brass and look almost like a weapon of war rather than a musical instrument.

But in case it may be thought that this vast instrument is just a freak, it is as well to know that Debussy in his *Iberia*, Wagner in his *Parsifal*, Ravel in *Ma Mère L'Oye* and Brahms in his *First Symphony* all used it and thought very highly of it.

It is not really an instrument for young players, unless perhaps they happen to have inherited one.

If they did and wanted some music for it, they might look up Mahler's *Symphony No. 9* or Strauss' *Electra*.

It sounds an octave lower than even the lowest note on the bassoon—and that is the very last note but one on the piano. Although not strictly speaking a transposing instrument, the notes for it are written an octave higher than they sound in order to avoid a bewildering number of ledger lines below the staff.

16 The Saxophone

There is a whole family of saxophones —the soprano, the alto, the tenor, the baritone, the bass. There are even a sopranino and a contrabass. However, only the alto, tenor and baritone are much used today. All are transposing instruments—that is, sounding a note other than the one written, as explained in the chapter on clarinet.

From being an obscure military band instrument, invented by a Belgian instrument maker, Adolphe Sax, in 1846, it has become one of the best known and most played members of the woodwind family, mostly because of its success in the world of jazz music, where its heavy sonorous, powerful tone is particularly well suited to the job.

The saxophone was originally an instrument used by Belgian military bands

It is a hybrid instrument, using the conical bore of the oboe family with the single reed of the clarinet family. It is NOT a brass instrument, despite the fact that it is made of brass. As has been said elsewhere in this book, it is not the material of which an instrument is made that categorizes it, but the method of producing sound on it. A brass instrument is one in which the sound is made by the vibrations of the lips held against a cup-shaped mouthpiece. All other blown instruments, are woodwind.

Adolphe Sax, who was a clarinettist as well as an instrument maker, felt that there was too big a gap in tonal quality between the normal woodwind and the brass. His invention, actually patented in 1846, was intended to combine the qualities of both groups of instruments. A rival military band leader, Sarrus, attempted to emulate the saxophone's success by producing a conical-bore instrument made of brass but with a double reed like the oboe and bassoon. He called it the sarrusophone and was immediately sued by Sax, who claimed he had pirated his ideas. Sax lost his case, but the sarrusophone eventually vanished.

The saxophone soon became a prized member of the wind band but, except for a few attempts by such composers as Bizet (*L'Arlesienne*), Debussy (*Rhapsodie*) and Jaques Ibert (*Concertino da Camera*) it made little impact on the symphony orchestra. Its great leap forward came with the jazz era of the 1920s, and since then it has produced a long list of brilliant players—Johnny Hodges, Harry Carney, Jimmy Dorsey, Charlie Parker, Benny Carter, Gerry Mulligan, John Coltrane and Tubby Hayes, to mention but a few. Saxophone parts in the works of serious composers include those in Strauss' *Symphonia Domestica*, Honegger's *Joan of Arc*, Vaughan Williams' *Sixth Symphony*,

Milhaud's *La Creation du Monde* and Ravel's *Bolero*. Despite this, however, the saxophone's true metier is probably the jazz group or pop group, where its powerful tone, agility and relative ease of playing, make it the perfect instrument for the job.

As a detail of passing interest, it has often been noticed that the shape of the bass clarinet resembles that of the saxophone. This is not surprising, since it was Adolphe Sax who gave the bass clarinet its present form.

The fingering of all the various sizes and pitches of saxophone is identical— a player can switch from one to the other with no more trouble than that necessary to adjust this embouchure to the different-sized mouthpiece. At one time there was a C Melody saxophone, which was non-transposing and was a great help in the days before every orchestration had properly transposed parts for the E-flat alto, the E-flat baritone (an octave lower) and the B-flat tenor (in between).

One of the features which helps to make the instrument easier to play is that there are no 'open holes' to be covered by the fingers, as in some other woodwind instruments. Unless the hole is perfectly closed there is a tendency for the instrument to 'overblow' or squeak. On all sizes of saxophone the holes are covered by leather- or nylon-covered pads held down by round metal keys. The player's finger presses down the metal key or a lever which actuates the key. Although the key system of a saxophone looks nightmarishly complicated, it is most skilfully designed to let the keys and levers fall naturally under the fingers— even small fingers. All the currently used saxophones (alto, tenor, baritone) are held by a sling round the player's neck, the instrument being steadied by the right-hand thumb on a thumb rest at the back of the instrument.

The alto in E flat

The baritone in E flat

The tenor in B flat

The bass in B flat

Playing position of the
alto saxophone

17 The Recorder

The recorder is the easiest of all instruments to *sound* but very hard to master. This is because it produces its notes by the player blowing through a whistle-type mouthpiece—there is neither reed nor cup mouthpiece, merely a sharp edge over which the stream of air is blown. The edge, or plug (called a fipple) disturbs the even blowing and thus vibrates the column of air within the instrument. The difficulty lies in the fact that the pressure of air must be exactly right—too little and there is no sound, the instrument will not 'speak', as they say; too much and it squeaks or jumps an octave.

When properly played, the recorder has a soft, mellow, sweet sound, which is most pleasing, either by itself or with other instruments of the same kind. It is not often used as an orchestral instrument and is happiest when it is grouped with other recorders.

It has a conical bore, eight holes and no keys (except on the larger instruments). The fingers must 'cover' properly, otherwise there is a squeak.

It has, of course, a long history. The early instrument was just a simple wooden tube which has been modified over the years. Shakespeare mentioned it in several of his plays and in the sixteenth century it was a fashionable instrument, wealthy families having 'chests' or 'sets' of anything from half-a-dozen to a couple of dozen recorders of various sizes. Friends used to gather at one another's houses for an evening of singing and recorder playing.

Around the 1700s, Jacques Hotteterre, grandson of the man who invented the modern oboe and bassoon, greatly improved the primitive recorder which had uneven tone and intonation (tuning). Suddenly it became popular with the great composers, Bach and Handel wrote for it and there were even sonatas specially composed for it.

One of the things that troubled composers of that period was the limited range of the recorder. But that was soon fixed by having recorders of various sizes, so that only the best part of each instrument's register was used. This extension of the 'family' reached absurd lengths, going from a tiny instrument barely 8 inches long to a super giant over 8 *feet* long. Today, the recorder family consists of five instruments—the sopranino, the descant (or soprano), the treble (or alto), the tenor, and the bass. The bass

Elizabethan recorder player

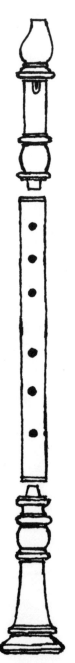

Parts of the recorder

is about 3 feet long and has a curved pipe at the top end into which the player blows. The most popular are the descant and treble.

The absence of keys would appear to make the instrument easier to play and so it does to a certain extent. But notes in the upper register have to be 'faked' by half-closing or 'pinching' the thumb hole.

For about a hundred years the recorder was very popular especially after Hotteterre had improved it. Bach included it in his *Brandenburg Concerto No. 4* with fast running passages.

Then suddenly it was eclipsed by the more brilliant sounding transverse flute. The recorder's soft mellow tones had blended well with the viols and the harpsichord but was unable to hold its own against the more powerful violins and piano which were coming into use. They existed side by side for a while and then for the next 150 years the recorder survived only in odd corners of the world doing odd jobs and in modified forms, such as the three-hole pipe found in the mountainous districts of Spain and France. This was played at village dances by a single musician who fingered the recorder with one hand and beat a tabor or small drum with the other. Other 'poor relations' which survived were the flageolet and the tin whistle.

In 1906 a French-Swiss, Arnold Dolmetsch, acquired an eighteenth-century Bressan recorder and became much interested in the playing of this instrument. Its loss in 1918 led Dolmetsch to start making the first modern recorders, based on the Bressan model. Soon its low cost, ease of playing and cool mellow sound caught on. Groups of music lovers formed

For boys and girls

themselves into recorder bands, old music was revived and new music written and published. The recorder was back!

In particular, schools took it up as a means of introducing music to children.

These are very attractive instruments and a very good way to start instrumental playing. But a word of warning is necessary perhaps; the recorders are unlike any other instruments in their fingering and blowing and should be regarded only as a starting point in learning other woodwind. The orchestral disciplines and reading of straightforward, untransposed music are, of course, the same as for other wind instruments and provide an extremely valuable grounding.

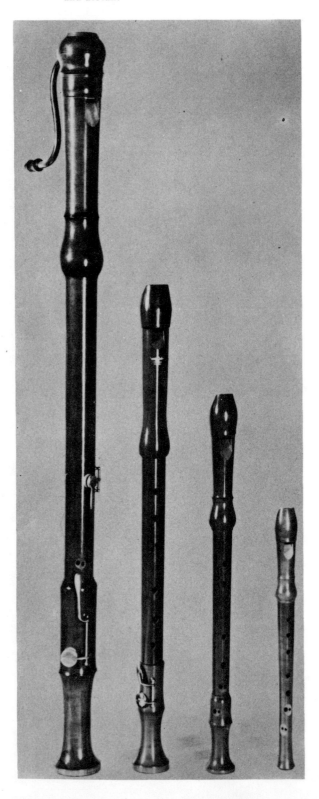

Family of recorders—bass, treble, tenor and descant

A helping pair of hands

18 The Trumpet and Cornet

What is the difference between the trumpet and cornet? They look very much alike and they sound very much alike, yet they have completely different roles. Why?

Well, they have different backgrounds, for a start. The trumpet is by far the older, going back to the ram's horn of biblical times, developing a different-shaped bore slowly over the centuries. The cornet 'arrived' complete in the 1820s. They do, of course, have many points in common—they are both brass instruments, they both have valves, the method of playing is almost identical.

But the cornet has a cone-shaped mouthpiece; the trumpet mouthpiece is hemispherical. The bore (internal shape) of the cornet is one-third cylindrical and two-thirds conical; the trumpet one-third conical and two-thirds cylindrical. These differences are not particularly striking from the outside (except that the cornet tends to be short and fat and the trumpet long and slender) but make a noticeable difference to the tone—and it is here that the really important difference lies.

The tone of the cornet tends to be thicker and rounder; the tone of the trumpet is brighter.

Both instruments are very flexible and can execute runs, leaps, trills, high tones, low tones. Both have the same range—about two-and-a-half octaves, although virtuoso players can extend this upwards to a most remarkable degree, the 'scream' trumpet of some of the modern jazz units taking it up a further octave or even more.

The cornet is a descendant of the post horn, which had a similar internal shape, but was without valves.

From its very early days in the mid-nineteenth century, the cornet was a favourite of brass virtuosi and it is still the most popular instrument for brass bands and some military bands, where its flexibility and 'easy speaking' make it ideal for florid solos like Arban's *Carnival of Venice*, as well as for slow melodic pieces. There is a long-model cornet, which looks so like a standard trumpet that only the expert eye can tell them apart. But its bore still makes it a cornet.

Some players switch mouthpieces, play-

The B flat cornet

The B flat trumpet

Brass on the march

ing a trumpet with the cornet mouthpiece on which they have learned. This makes changing the embouchure (method of pursing the lips to produce the right vibrations) unnecessary but tends to blur the trumpet's natural brilliance.

Many players of the trumpet started on the cornet, and it is sometimes erroneously stated that the cornet is an 'easier' instrument for the beginner to start on. If the player intends to go in for symphony orchestra work, or dance bands, or jazz units, then he should start on the trumpet right from the very beginning and get his embouchure 'set' as soon as possible.

It was explained in Chapter 4 how the valves on brass instruments alter the pitch of the notes by adding short lengths of tubing. In the old days before valves were invented the trumpet players got their notes by playing right at the top of the register where the harmonics are so close together that a continuous scale can be played.

Harmonics are the notes which are produced by the column of air, or string, vibrating in sections, as explained in Chapter 3. When the whole length vibrates it produces the 'fundamental' or No. 1 harmonic; vibrating in halves produces the No. 2 harmonic, an octave higher; the next harmonic produces a note five notes higher; the next is four notes higher; the next is three notes higher; the next is two-and-a-half notes higher. And so on until the notes make a complete scale. Earlier trumpet players had to be very expert at using these adjacent harmonics, and did so for Bach's rapid trumpet passages in his *Brandenburg Concerto No. 2.*

The invention of the valve in 1815 changed the whole aspect of trumpet playing and the shape and length of the instrument. Any of the harmonics can be produced by the use of the valves on a brass instrument, as they can by the holes on a wind instrument, or by lightly touching the strings of a violin, viola, cello or bass.

There are many pitches of trumpet (E-flat, D, C, B-flat, and F): a bass trumpet in C similar to a valve trombone, and cornet (E-flat soprano, B-flat) but the B-flat instruments are standard, the others being used for special works. Both the cornet and trumpet have a wide range of mutes of metal or fibre, which alter the tone or reduce the volume, the more extreme of them being reserved for jazz playing.

Haydn, Shostakovich and others wrote concertos for the trumpet and there are beautiful solos in the Bach B minor Mass, Handel's *Messiah* ('The Trumpet Shall Sound') and *Water Music*, the Sibelius *Symphony No. 2*, and in almost all the works of Wagner and Strauss. Janacek's *Sinfonietta* is a good example of the sound of the trumpet with full orchestral brass. One of the best-known pieces is the *Trumpet Voluntary* by Jeremiah Clarke, often wrongly attributed to Purcell.

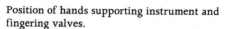

The trumpet 'embouchure'

Position of hands supporting instrument and fingering valves.

Playing position for the trumpet

Bach or 'herald's' trumpet

An oliphant (old English for 'elephant'). An ivory hunting horn, in use from around 800 A.D.

19 The Trombone

Playing position for the tenor trombone

The trombone
'embouchure'

Position of the hands

The old English name for the trombone was sackbut, which came from two French words meaning *push-pull*, which is just how the trombonist plays his instrument.

Ancient as the trombone is—and it goes back in its present form to the 1400s —it did not exist in biblical times, although the phrase in the Book of Daniel 3:

> 'That at what time ye hear the sound of the cornet, flute, harp, sackbut. . . .'

seems to suggest that it did. In fact the instrument at Nebuchadnezzar's feast was not of the trombone type but a form of harp, centuries of translation and re-translation having altered the meaning.

The trombone began to evolve from the old-time trumpet, at the time when that instrument was built in various sizes in order to extend the range of the family 'voice'. Some unknown genius thought of bending the nine-foot tube of the bass trumpet back on itself and inserting a section which slid in and out, thus giving the trombone, alone among the brass instruments of the period, the capability of playing all notes of the scale. The word 'trombone' is Italian for 'big trumpet'.

Its tube is cylindrical for most of its length, broadening out at the end to form a bell eight or nine inches across. The mouthpiece is like a large trumpet mouthpiece and the player produces the sound in exactly the same way—by tensing his lips and forcing air through them so that they vibrate and set the column of air inside the instrument also vibrating.

The trombonist must have a very good ear. As he pushes and pulls the slide in and out there are no keys or frets or other markings to guide him—he has to bring the slide to rest at the precise spot otherwise the note is out of tune. In modern dance and jazz trombone playing the player wavers the slide back and forth to produce a vibrato like that of the violin, but this technique is not used in the symphony orchestra except very occasionally for a special effect.

Trombones began to become popular with composers from the early 1600s, Monteverdi using them to great effect in his opera *Orfeo*. They grew in favour in the fields of opera, oratorios and masses and the trombone was a standard instrument in church orchestras until well into the nineteenth century, but did not take hold in the concert orchestra until the early 1800s. Gluck used them in his opera also called *Orfeo*. Mozart followed with his *Don Giovanni*, using three trombones with great effect for the graveyard scene. Beethoven also called for three trombones in his *Fifth Symphony*, and Brahms, Wagner and Strauss used the instrument frequently. More modern composers like Hindemith, Rimsky-Korsakov and Milhaud have written concertos for the instrument. A notable example of the use

Sackbut player

of the trombone is in 'March to the Scaffold' for Berlioz' *Symphonie Fantasque*.

There are several pitches of trombone —the treble trombone (which is really a slide trumpet and now virtually obsolete), the B-flat tenor trombone (the standard instrument today) and the bass trombone in G, or in F and E-flat. The bass trombone is today very largely superseded by a hybrid instrument called the tenor-bass (sometimes just called the tenor trombone in B-flat and F).

This last-named instrument has the

Glenn Miller

pitch of a tenor trombone but the bore of a bass, and has a so-called 'F attachment', a system of extra tubing which gives the instrument an additional three feet or so of tubing and another four lower notes. The F attachment is cut in by the player pressing a lever with his left thumb. Yet another note is produced with what is called an E slide. A still more complicated version has still another lever which adds further low notes.

The 'true' bass trombone in G is still used and can be recognized by the extension handle attached to the slide to enable the player to stretch out to the bottom positions on the slide. There is also a tenor *valve* trombone, without a slide, which is really a bass trumpet, but this is not much used.

The trombone has a beautiful mellow tone, very sweet in its top register—the famous band leader Tommy Dorsey made

a speciality of playing soft-and-sweet at the very top of the register and convinced listeners that the trombone need not blast the eardrums (although it can, if so desired!).

In the early days of ragtime, the bands of New Orleans used to ride to funerals and other events on a farm wagon. Because the trombonist needed room for his slide, he was placed at the back of the wagon, near the tail gate or drop-down section at the back. Thus trombonists who play in the New Orleans jazz style are known today as 'tail-gate' trombonists.

One of the characteristics of the trombone, which can soon be monotonous if over-used, is the glissando—a sliding from one note to the next created by moving the slide slowly and continuously through its range and blowing all the time.

Right Bass trombone in G

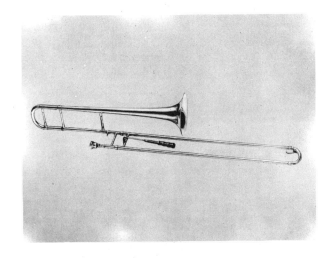

Below right Tenor trombone in B flat

Below Tenor-bass trombone in B flat and F

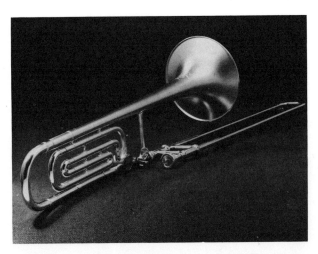

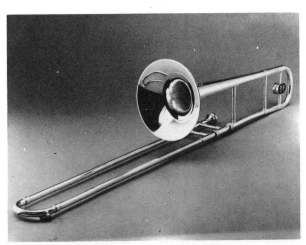

20 The Flugel Horn, Tenor Horn, Baritone, Euphonium and Bass

Playing position for the flugel horn

All these instruments are band instruments and are therefore considered together as a group. The flugel horn is currently having a vogue among pop groups and jazz units, and the bass is frequently met with in the symphony orchestra, but the rest of them keep to their own world or the brass and military bands.

All are, of course, brass instruments within the definition of method of sound-production—i.e. pursed lips and a cup mouthpiece.

Brass bands are to be found all over the world but probably reach their highest peak of musical skill in the North of England. Their composition varies somewhat, but they always include cornets plus all these instruments listed at the head of this page, trombones and percussion. The military band is more varied in its composition and includes some of the above plus woodwind and percussion.

One of the problems in considering these groups is that the instruments have

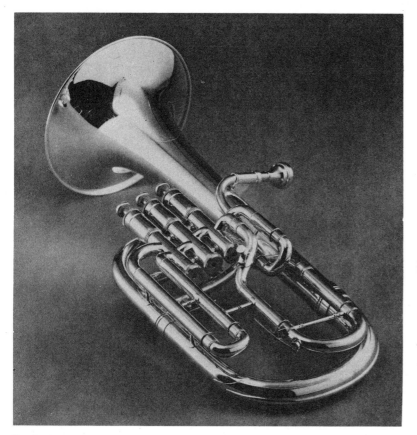

Euphonium

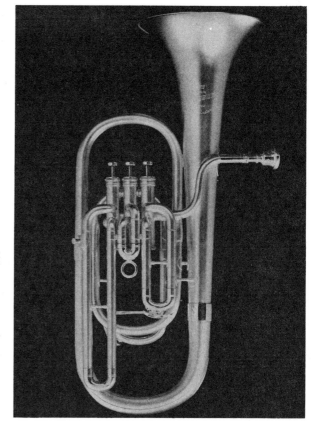

Baritone

BB flat bass   EE flat bass

E flat Tenor Horn

so many different names. Classified as the saxhorn family (though in fact this is a name not much used now) from the fact that they owe their present form to the indefatigable Adolphe Sax mentioned earlier, and the flugel horn family (of which only one example currently survives), the saxhorns all have their bells pointing upwards, and only the flugel horns have them pointing forwards. However, both families have valves like the cornet and trumpet and both are built on the bugle model with conical bores. The saxhorns and flugel horns have very wide bores and it is this wideness of bore which gives all these instruments their thick heavy tone.

First in the brass band range is the cornet. After that comes the flugel horn in B-flat. It is like a rather fat cornet but with a thicker voice. Next comes the tenor horn in E-flat and it is this one that has the most names—saxhorn, alto saxhorn, tenor, tenor saxhorn, tenor horn, alto, althorn and even a circular model called a tenor cor.

Getting further down the musical scale, we come next to the B-flat baritone (also called the tenor in B-flat, althorn in B-flat, baritone saxhorn), then to the B-flat euphonium, which might be described as the cello of the brass band.

Finally come the basses, of which there is quite a range. First there is the E-flat bass, then the B-flat bass (a fifth lower), then the EE-flat bass and the BB-flat bass (the double letter signifying merely that the tubing is wide, giving a heavier tone). All these are also called tubas (and so is the euphonium, which is sometimes called the tenor tuba). The E-flat bass is identical with the orchestral tuba. There was still another version of the brass

basses called a circular bass—the main body of the instrument being built in a kind of giant hoop to go round the player's body, being supported on his shoulder. The first versions of these were called helicons. Sousa, the great American band conductor, had one constructed so that the bell deflected the sound forward. This was called the sousaphone.

The basses are truly majestic instruments, having mouthpieces of getting on for two inches in diameter. But contrary to all the jokes made in the newspapers at the times of band contests they do not require an over amount of wind. The embouchure (pursing of the lips) and length of tubing make the noise, not a great deal of puffing and blowing, although undoubtedly they require more wind than the smaller saxhorns. But young people can play them without difficulty.

Wagner liked the tubas so much that he had some specially made with a slightly narrower bore (and therefore brighter tone) and were a cross between a tuba and a French horn, using French horn-type mouthpieces. Both a tenor and a bass model and were used in *The Ring of the Nibelungs*. They were also used by Bruckner and Richard Strauss.

Some of the euphoniums and basses have a fourth valve to extend the range downwards.

Music for the range of saxhorns can mostly be found in the brass band repertoire, but there are tuba solos in Moussorgsky's *Pictures from an Exhibition*, and Vaughan Williams wrote a concerto for the tuba which is quite often performed and demonstrates that the instrument, however ungainly, is capable of a great deal more than oom-pahs.

21 The French Horn

The lur, an old Danish instrument, with a very ancient lineage going back to Egyptian and Babylonian times

Of all the instruments of the orchestra, the French horn probably looks the most complicated and is often said to be the most difficult to play.

Yet its direct ancestor was one of the simplest of prehistoric instruments—the curved, short animal horn which, with the tip sawn or broken off, could be made to give out one or two rough sounds—hardly even notes. Such horns were the ancestor of the Greek and Roman wooden and metal instruments to be seen in frescoes and reliefs, but the craft of making and curving metal tubes was lost with the fall of the Roman Empire and only gradually rediscovered during the Middle Ages, when the simple horn was used extensively as a signalling instrument, not only for military purposes, but also on the hunting field.

The conch shell was similarly adapted as an instrument and is often shown in depictions of the classical sea gods. When played, this mediaeval horn was held with the bell end curving up in front of the player's face.

The instrument attracted the attention of composers of the seventeenth century, always on the lookout for new 'colours' to add to their orchestral palette. After

Ifor James, famous French horn player

'Stopping' by inserting right hand into the bell

Left hand supporting the instrument and operating valves

Playing position for the French horn

changing the shape of the instrument from the big single hoop to two smaller ones, the horn found a regular place in the orchestras of the late seventeenth century. But, like the bugle, it could sound only its 'open' notes. A skilful player of the period could get extra notes by tightening or slackening his lips and by inserting his fingers into the wide bell of the instrument, which not only raised or lowered the notes by half a tone, but changed the quality of the sound as well. But if he wanted to get a completely new range of notes, he had to add 'crooks' (short, curved pieces of tubing) to the body of the instrument.

The invention of valves changed all this, as it did for the trumpet. But the 'natural' horn, as it was called, did not die immediately. Composers still liked the tone of the older instrument. By the 1900s, however, the valve horn had taken over completely and was used in two sizes—in F and in B-flat. Today the two horns are often combined in one instrument, the valve tubes being duplicated and operated from a single set of rotary valves with a thumb-operated fourth valve to switch the horn from F to B-flat and vice versa.

It is a conical-bore instrument, starting off at a quarter of an inch at the mouthpiece and gradually swelling throughout its 17 feet to a widely flared bell of some eleven to fourteen inches. The mouthpiece is funnel-shaped and unlike any other brass instrument mouthpiece. Because of this extreme length and narrow bore, the instrument is particularly susceptible to changes of temperature and humidity. The player must always warm up his instrument and even if he does, he

The single horn   The half-double horn   The full double horn

cannot be sure of not 'splitting' a note.

The range of the French horn is three-and-a-half octaves, although not all the notes in the low register are practicable, and it is a transposing instrument—that is, it sounds a note other than that written. One of the oddities of the instrument is its name. The English thought it had come from France and called it the French horn, but the French thought it had come from Germany and called it the German horn.

To add further complication to an already very complicated instrument, the old technique of inserting the hand into the bell, although no longer necessary for the original reason of producing extra notes, is still used to change the mellow tone of the horn into a thin, distant sound which can be very exciting when used at the right moment. But putting the hand right into the bell puts the note out of tune by a semitone, so the player has to compensate for this by transposing mentally down a semitone. Some horns have an extra valve which does this automatically.

As well as this hand 'stopping', as it is called, the instrument can be muted by metal or cardboard mutes. Another effect sometimes called for by composers is *pavillon en l'air*, which means lifting the bell up into the air so that the sound comes out loud and unhindered. Mahler uses this trick in his *Symphony No. 4.*

In order to meet individual preferences, instrument manufacturers produce a wide variety of horns. The simplest version is one pitched in F only, but usually supplied with a separate tuning slide to convert it to E-flat for simpler fingering in certain keys, and fitted with piston valves like those of a trumpet. In addition to this there is the 'half double' horn, a somewhat confusing term indicating that it converts from F to B-flat by means of a fourth valve, but does not have two separate sets of valve tubes.

Finally, there is 'full double' horn, which has everything, including an extra slide to convert to E-flat as well as a valve to switch it from F to B-flat.

Peter and the Wolf uses three French horns to indicate the wolf and beautiful examples of horn usage can be heard in Mendelssohn's *Midsummer Night's Dream* and the famous Siegfried theme of Wagner's *The Ring*. The horn is given an important solo by Shostakovitch in his *Fifth Symphony*, and the composer directs that a certain high note shall be played only if the performer can play it very quietly—otherwise it is to be played an octave lower!

The pop drummer

22 The Timpani

Several times in this book the ancient lineage of many of the instruments has been mentioned. But none can compare with the history of the percussion family. 'Drumming'—whether beating two pieces of wood together or merely clapping the hands—is surely as old as man himself.

Percussion means 'hitting'—therefore all instruments which are hit are grouped together under that general title, although this does not allow for instruments like the piano or dulcimer where the strings are hit with hammers.

The principal percussion instruments are the timpani. Of all the orchestral drums they are the only ones which sound a definite note. These notes are generated by the size and tension of the skin, and are amplified by the copper or fibreglass bowls under them. There is a limit to how much the heads can be tightened, however, and the range is extended by having drums of different diameters. Thus, the minimum for orchestral use is two timpani, 25 and 28 inches in diameter, but often composers call for three, four, five or even more, adding 23 and 30 inches to the sizes mentioned above. The pitch of the note is changed by tightening or loosening the tension on the head. In the simple form of timpani this is accomplished by several turn-screws pulling down a ring which in its turn pulls down the hoop that holds taut the calfskin or plastic head. In some instruments there is only one handle, the others being turned by connecting rods and pulleys. The most elaborate form of timpani have pedals which the player depresses or releases by foot pressure. These are called 'pedal timpani' or 'machine-tuning timpani'. Strange glissando effects can be got by using the pedal to change the tension of the drumhead, playing continuously at the same time.

Tomorrow's timpanists? Young percussion players in a junior school percussion band

The name needs a little explanation. The English word is 'kettledrums' but this is used less than the Italian word 'timpani'. But note that it is NOT spelt 'tympani', and that it is plural; one drum is a 'timpano'. Musicians usually call them 'timps' in the plural and 'a timp' in the singular.

At one time the timpani were tuned to only two notes—the tonic and dominant (that is, the first note of the scale and the fifth). At those parts of the music where these particular notes did not fit the timpani remained silent. Later on, timpanists had to learn the difficult trick of re-tuning during the course of a symphony or other piece of music.

The tuning of the timpani calls for not only a very exact ear but the power to shut out all other noises except the one

it is wished to hear. The timpanist has to change the tuning of his instruments while the orchestra is playing and whether he does this with hand-tuning or pedal-tuning, you will see him with his head bent over the head, tapping gently and listening for the exact tuning even when the orchestra is playing in a different key.

The timpanist uses cane-handled sticks with heads (usually made of felt) of various degrees of hardness for different effects. The drumhead has to be very carefully struck, not at the centre but half-way between the centre and the rim, otherwise the skin would 'choke' and not give a clear sound. The sticks have to be quickly withdrawn after striking for the same reasons and sometimes the sound has to be 'damped' by a quick touch of the timpanist's hand.

Playing position for the timpani

Pedal tuning timpani

The effect of a sustained note is obtained by the 'roll', produced by a very rapid alternating beat.

Timpani are capable of a very great range of volume, from a whispering softness to a veritable bashing which can almost drown out the entire orchestra.

Since Haydn wrote passages for solo timpani in his *Symphony No. 103*, solos have become quite common. The invention of pedal-tuning made the timpani even more useful in this respect. Schumann's *Symphony No. 6* is a very fine example. Stravinsky used five timpani in his *Rite of Spring* and asks for five players (he usually gets three). Holst, in his *The Planets*, wrote a solo for four timpani, to be played by one performer. The extreme was perhaps reached by Berlioz in his *Requiem*, for which sixteen drums and ten timpanists are required.

A very unusual effect is the glissando (a sliding from one note to the next without pause), which can only be done on the machine-tuning drums. Bartók used this in his *Music for Strings, Percussion and Celesta*.

Timpani are only used in orchestras, bands, and occasionally in large dance bands. The timpanist is the leader of the percussion group when there are several players. In orchestras with fewer players, one player often handles all the percussion instruments.

23 The Drums

'The drums' covers quite a number of instruments. In one sense it refers only to the snare drum and bass drum with their attendant accessories. In another it is the generic term for all the percussion instruments—timpani, vibraphone and everything else.

The component parts of the more precise meaning of the term are (a) the bass drum, (b) the snare drum, (c) the bass drum pedal, (d) tom-toms, (e) cymbals, (f) gong, (g) tambourine and castanets, (h) miscellaneous sticks, beaters, stands, brackets, etc.

The bass drum used in the jazz unit or pop group is usually about 22 inches in diameter by 17 inches deep. It stands on its side and is played by a foot pedal beating against one head. In the symphony orchestra it is much larger, up to 36 inches or more, and is played resting on a stand, the player using one felt-covered stick. In marching bands, it is carried on the chest of the player, who uses two sticks. Whichever way it is used, the effect is the same—a deep powerful sound without definite pitch, that provides a steady rhythmic foundation.

Wire brushes on the snare drum

Nigerian drummers

The snare drum is usually 14 by 6 inches, has much thinner heads, and a dozen or so wires (snares) stretched tautly against the lower head, which rattle against the head and produce the characteristic 'snap' of the instrument. It is played with two wooden sticks. The snares can be lifted clear of the head to produce a tom-tom effect.

The tom-toms belong to the jazz unit or beat group and will not be found in the symphony orchestra, except for special effects, nor in the brass band. They have two heads but no snares, and their sizes can be anything from 12 by 8 inches to 16 by 16 inches. The smaller ones are usually attached to the bass drum, the larger being supported on their own stands. The number used depends on the preferences of the performer and there can be up to six or more tom-toms of various sizes.

This applies equally to cymbals. At least two are standard, but possibly several will be used, all of different sizes and tones. A special device is the 'hi-hat' cymbals and stand, which consists of two cymbals turned to face one another, and mounted on a stand with a pedal. Operation of the pedal brings the two cymbals together with a sharply-cut-off 'zip' and is mostly used on the offbeat to balance the bass drum on the onbeat. 'Sizzle' cymbals, which produce a buzzing effect through loose metal inserts in the surface of the cymbal, are another occasionally used device. The symphony orchestra also uses cymbals but in a very different way.

The drummer uses a variety of sticks and beaters, including a pair of wire brushes, which produce a rhythmic 'swishing' noise when stroked against the snare drum, tom-toms or cymbals.

In addition to the foregoing there is an almost endless number of other devices —triangles, cowbells, tambourines, wood block, castanets and so on, all of which may be required to be played by the drummer at some time.

The functions of drummers in the various kinds of musical units vary widely. In the symphony orchestras and in brass and military bands each instrument of the drummer's array is written for exactly and the performer sticks closely to the written part. In the dance bands, jazz units and pop groups seldom is the drum part more than a mere skeleton guide, the player's skill being displayed in the extemporizations he creates as he goes along. These two different styles of playing affect the instruments used, not only in their shape and design (e.g. the bass drum in the symphony orchestra and its counterpart in the pop group are

widely different) but the manner in which they are used.

The intending drummer, therefore, must know beforehand what kind of drumming he intends to do and buy his kit accordingly. The pop group 'outfit' would be completely out of place in the symphony orchestra and vice versa.

For the intending symphony orchestra or general orchestral player a knowledge of music is essential. The proper learning of the various percussion instruments is equally important, otherwise the player will not be able to play the parts that are put in front of him. The famous snare drum solo in Ravel's *Bolero* is a case in point—it is difficult for a trained player, almost impossible for an untrained one.

On the other hand, players in jazz units and pop groups often are self-taught and quite brilliant in their extemporizations. A few of these players are academy trained, but the majority are not and would be lost with an orchestral part.

Tuned tom-toms—sounding different but indeterminate notes

24 The Xylophone and Vibraphone

The xylophone consists of a series of wooden bars, graded, shaped and sized to produce a scale of notes when struck. An essential part of its construction is that the bars shall be able to vibrate freely and they are therefore either suspended on cords or supported in some other way so that the vibrations are not dampened by contact with the structure.

Its origin goes back to primitive man, who drew different sounds from different sized slabs of wood or stone. By the Middle Ages an instrument had evolved made either of wood or glass, and graduated and tuned to a modern scale. At this stage it looked like a ladder, the bars being threaded on a string, held up in the left hand and struck by a hammer in the right. Later the 'ladder' was laid flat on a stand and resonators (long metal tubes matched to the size of the bars) suspended underneath the bars in order to increase the volume.

A South American version of this, using very large bars, is called a marimba, and is sometimes so large that it can

A school xylophone

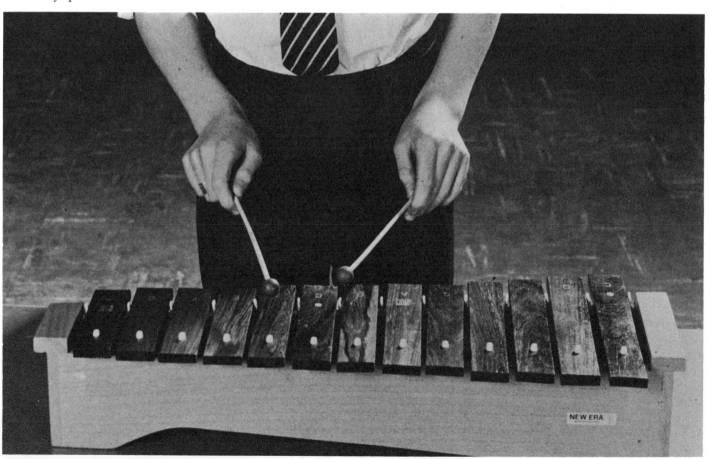

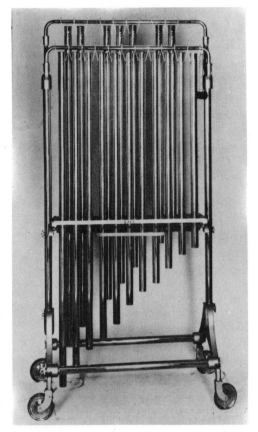

Triangle and beater

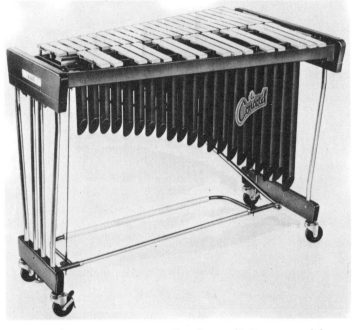

1½-octave chromatic tubular bells with hand-operated damper

3-octave vibraphone with foot-operated damper

accommodate several players sitting side by side. An orchestral version of the marimba, which has bars several times the size of those used for xylophones, is sometimes seen in large modern orchestras. It is played with soft felt beaters and has a mellow, round sound, very different from the hard, dry rattle of the xylophone.

Saint-Saëns used this latter sound to great effect in his *Danse Macabre* when it was supposed to represent the sound of skeletons dancing! It also represents the fossils in the *Carnival of Animals*.

Other composers who have used the xylophone are Bartók (*Music for Strings, Percussion and Celesta*), Shostakovich (*Fifth Symphony*) and Copland (*Music for the Theatre*).

Miniature xylophones, usually without resonators, are used by children's percussion bands.

First cousin to the xylophone is the glockenspiel, which is exactly the same in every way except that its bars are made of metal and not resonated. Its tone is very high-pitched, silvery and penetrating. It is usually played with hard wooden hammers, which accentuate its tone.

Debussy wrote for the glockenspiel in his *La Mer*, and Mahler used it in his *Symphony No. 4*. There are some glockenspiels played from a piano keyboard, but their tone is inferior to that of the hand-beaten instrument. The keyboard glockenspiel should not be confused with the celesta, which is a much more elaborate affair and although it resembles a miniature piano in appearance, is actually a percussion instrument, the keys operating hammers which strike resonated metal bars and give a light, feathery, delicate sound. Another kind of glockenspiel, very popular with marching bands, is that mounted on a pole held in one hand, and played with a hammer in the other.

About the 1930s, the humble glocken-

Tambourine and hand cymbals

Gary Burton, vibraphone virtuoso

spiel was developed into an entirely new instrument called the vibraphone (or, in common usage, 'the vibes'). The metal bars of the glockenspiel were enlarged to many times their size, and each bar had a tubular resonator placed under it. But the major development was that each resonator had a kind of revolving lid at the top end, which was turned by an electric motor. As the lid was 'open', the note produced was echoing and mellow; as it was closed the tone became dry and flat. The rapid alternation between these two produced the characteristic wavering sound of the instrument. This has often been likened to the vibrato produced by the string player but it is in fact quite different—the violinist slightly sharpens and flattens the note by rolling his finger back and forth, whereas the vibraphone merely alternates between echo and non-echo.

The instrument has become enormously popular with light orchestra and some modern composers. It is not, of course, to be found in classical compositions, which were written before it was invented. The most distinguished modern composer to have used the vibraphone is Boulez.

To complete this chapter mention should be made of the tubular bells. These are hollow tubes of steel, up to 1 or 2 inches in diameter and varying from 3 to 5 feet long. Their effect is similar to that of a church bell. The tubular bells are included in the kit of the all-purpose percussion player and are played by striking them near the top with a rawhide mallet. They were used to great effect in Tchaikovsky's *1812 Overture*, along with the cannon-firing, to produce the sound of a city in the midst of battle with the church bells chiming and clashing.

25 The Piano

Artur Rubinstein

In 1709 Bartolommeo Cristofori, the curator of musical instruments for the fabulously wealthy Medici family of Florence, proudly announced that he had invented a new instrument. He called it a *gravicembalo col piano e forte*—a keyboard instrument that can be played soft and loud. Today we know his instrument by the name of 'pianoforte', generally shortened to 'piano'.

The reason he called his invention by such a complicated name was that the keyboard instruments of the period, the harpsichord and clavichord, lacked dynamic range—that is, it was impossible to go from very soft to very loud, variation in finger touch having little or no effect. This was exactly what Cristofori's new instrument could do, so that is what he called it.

There was some dispute at the time, other instrument makers laying claim to have been first with the idea, but Cristofori is generally given the credit. And certainly he started a revolution.

Two of the new instruments were made and submitted to J. S. Bach for his opinion, but he did not think much of them. However, one of his sons, J. C. Bach, approved of the instrument, was the first person to perform in public on it and introduced it to Mozart, who became one of the first virtuosi of the pianoforte.

Early pianos were small, their sound light and delicate, but for public playing larger and more powerful instruments were needed and were soon provided. Mozart's piano had a range of less than five octaves; a piano built for Beethoven in 1817 had six octaves; today it is normal to have seven-and-a-quarter octaves—to be exact fifty-two white keys and thirty-six black ones.

Despite its comparative youth, the piano exceeds all other instruments in popularity. Its success in the home, in the concert hall, on radio and television, is based on the fact that it does not need the support of other instruments, whereas most other instruments sound happier in an ensemble. The only exception to this is the organ but, except in its small, electronic form, the organ is not suitable for the normal house and is impossible to transport.

The earliest pianos were shaped like the grand piano of today—that is, like a harp lying on its side. The keyboard was placed so that the player's hands were partially hidden, but as audiences wanted to watch the hands, instruments were designed to make this possible. Makers experimented with all sorts of shapes and sizes. One set a harp-shaped body on end to make a giant upright, nine feet high, called the giraffe piano. In 1800 a civil engineer called Hawkins invented the complete iron frame, and with it the upright piano. With the iron frame strings could be given much higher tension and this resulted in increased brilliance. In 1821 Erard invented the double-escapement, which meant that the hammer did not have to drop all the way back immediately after striking the string, thus making fast passages much easier to play. Over-stringing—that is, placing one set of strings over another—made it possible to decrease the size of the instrument while not sacrificing the length of the strings.

With the modifications to the form of the piano, the pattern of playing also changed. With skilful use of the sustaining pedal, Chopin showed how the piano could 'sing'; Liszt changed the low-seat-and-flat-forearm posture to a high-seat-and-sloping-forearm one and ranged up and down the keyboard with hitherto unheard-of virtuosity.

Some grand pianos have three pedals; one on the right called the 'loud' or sustaining pedal, which lifts all the dampers and allows the strings to continue sounding; one on the left, the 'soft' pedal, which moves the hammers so that the sound is softer than usual; one in the middle which lifts the dampers on certain strings. Upright pianos do not have this third or 'sostenuto' pedal.

The piano is used both for solo melodies and for accompaniments; each hand can play a separate melody; both single notes and chords are possible. It can suggest the melody lines of a whole orchestra, and many orchestral works have been

90

transcribed so that they can be played on the piano.

Clearly the piano is an instrument of almost infinite versatility. It can combine very happily with any other instrument and indeed does so in nearly all spheres of music.

Although not normally a member of the symphony orchestra, it will nevertheless often be found *with* it. Piano concertos are written for a virtuoso piano soloist playing with the orchestra, which sometimes acts as an accompaniment and sometimes plays an equal part. Examples are innumerable—Mozart's *Coronation Concerto*, written for the coronation of Leopold II; Beethoven's *Emperor Concerto*; concertos by Schumann, Brahms and Grieg. In the slow movement of Beethoven's Fourth Concerto, piano and orchestra play parts of equal importance and the same is true of D'Indy's *Symphony on a French Mountain Air* and de Falla's *Nights in the Gardens of Spain*.

The piano is also used as an orchestral instrument with orchestras smaller than the full symphony—light concert orchestras and the like. This is largely as twentieth-century development, although it had its first counterpart in the eighteenth century when the harpsichord player played from a skeleton part called a 'figured bass' or from the orchestral score, and had the task of filling in the weak places and holding the orchestra together. As the art of conducting developed in the early nineteenth century, so this usage died out. Modern examples of the use of the piano in the orchestra come from Stravinsky, who includes it in his *Suite for a Small Orchestra* and Messiaen, who introduces long and elaborate piano solos into many of his choral and orchestral works.

But these functions are far from being the total of the piano's versatility. It can ally itself with other solo instruments, as in Schumann's *Adagio and Allegro for Horn and Piano* and of course there are numerous piano trios, quartets and quintets.

The piano has always lent itself especially to solo work, and countless pieces

exist for solo piano, duets for two pianos and duets for four hands on one piano. Among outstanding composers for solo piano are Beethoven, Mozart, Schumann, Brahms, Chopin and Debussy; works by all of whom are readily available on records. Some composers have produced works for *one* hand only—Scriabin, Ravel and Strauss have written compositions for the left hand only and Alkan and others have written for the right hand alone.

One of the really important usages of the piano is, of course, as an accompanying instrument for solo instrumentalists and singers. This is an art on its own and one famous pianist, Gerald Moore, rose to fame and honour doing nothing else but accompanying the world's greatest singers and instrumentalists. His books about his experiences and about the techniques of accompanying should be read by all pianists.

Modern composers like Prokofiev, Boulez and Copland have written for the piano in a manner considerably different from the great classical composers of the past, tending to use it as an almost gong-like percussion instrument, full of powerful reverberations.

Modern virtuoso players such as Van Cliburn, Daniel Barenboim, Horowitz,

Action of a modern upright piano

Sviatoslav Richter and others use a nine-foot concert grand, which has a fast action and a powerful, booming bass.

John Cage, the American composer, uses what he calls a 'prepared' piano, which consists of an ordinary grand piano on the strings of which he puts nuts and bolts, bits of tin and other objects.

All this says nothing, of course, of the tremendous place the piano has in dance bands, jazz units and some pop groups (although the latter tend to use the electronic versions of the instrument as blending better with the amplified sound of their guitars).

Ever since the early days of jazz, the piano has been an essential instrument to the group. Players like Earl Hines, Duke Ellington, Fats Waller, Art Tatum, Teddy Wilson, Errol Garner, Nat King Cole and many more built an almost legendary repertoire of rhythmic piano playing, most of which is fortunately preserved on records.

We should not overlook, either, such performers as Liberace and Victor Borge who, although they are known more for their purely vaudeville entertainment, are concert pianists of considerable ability. The spangle-suited Liberace recently announced that he had been contracted to make a series of player-piano rolls, thus following in the footsteps of such illustrious performers as Grieg, Debussy and Percy Grainger, who 'cut' rolls of their own compositions. The player piano, in which the notes are operated by means of a perforated paper roll inserted into the instrument, was a great favourite in the 1930s, but died out with the advent of the juke box. Perhaps it is due for a revival—if so it may be a blessing to those who like 'playing' the piano but can't be bothered to learn how to!

There is also the electronic piano, using amplified vibrating reeds, shaped either like a mini-piano or small and easily portable. In most cases it has three or four different tones, ranging from standard piano to 'honky-tonk' piano or harpsichord, producible at the touch of a 'voice tab'.

Below Playing position for the piano

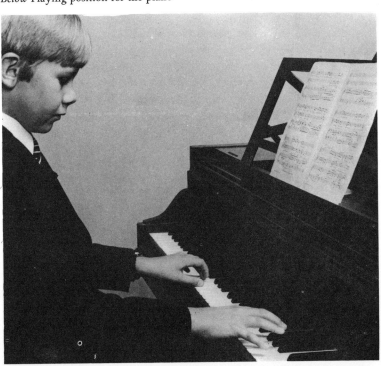

Below Electric piano

Mediaeval portable organ

Playing position for
the church organ

26 The Organ

The great organs of cathedral and concert hall are basically a collection of pipes, in number anything from a few hundred to several thousand, and varying in length from a few inches to 32 feet. Some of the pipes are pencil-thin, others are big enough for a man to crawl through. Some are like giant whistles (that is, the wind that is forced through them 'breaks' over a plug in the end), others have tongues which vibrate like the reeds of woodwind instruments.

The air supply comes nowadays from an electric pump; in earlier times and even now in some tiny country churches, it came from men or boys working a hand pump. The organist sits in front of a console which may contain anything up to six keyboards, another keyboard being played by the feet.

Each pipe of an organ can only sound one note and each pipe forms one of a larger group of pipes called a 'stop'. Each 'stop' is part of a *sectional organ* and each sectional organ is part of the *grand organ*. The pipes in each stop produce sounds of similar quality but, of course, of different pitches; and each stop is governed by a separate knob on the console. Each sectional organ has its own keyboard or manual.

The organ is an extremely difficult instrument to master, although playing the accompaniment to simple hymns in church presents no great problem. The reason for all the complication is, of course, to produce an almost infinite number of 'colours' and combinations of colours. Many of the stops sound like orchestral instruments, but although it is quite often used in conjunction with a symphony orchestra, the organ cannot

truly be called an orchestral instrument. It can and does stand alone, and is happier doing so. The range of organ music is tremendous, with Bach's great works, including the *Art of Fugue* perhaps heading the list.

The syrinx or panpipes, that small instrument of great antiquity, is the direct if distant forerunner of mighty instruments such as the world's largest organ, in Atlantic City, USA, which has two consoles with twelve manuals between them, 1,477 stops and 33,112 pipes! Today there is a tendency towards smaller pipe organs; the old ones are being repaired and renovated and new ones of a similar nature are being built.

Another kind of organ is also being

Grand Organ of the
Royal Festival
Hall, London

The Diamond
electronic organ

Two organ flue pipes.
The world's largest
organ, in Atlantic City,
U.S.A., has 33,112 pipes

developed—the electronic organ. This is not to be confused with the electrically blown organ, which goes back as far as 1864. The new instrument is completely electronic, with electrical circuits and amplifiers taking the place of pipes. This kind of organ has not only entered the home in competition with the piano (it takes up no more room and costs not much more) but also in many schools, churches and even concert halls, although some musicians are not entirely persuaded of its acceptability. These instruments work by a number of different methods. One of the most used is a rotating disc inserted between a light source and a photo-electric cell. Another is a controlled 'heterodyning', like the whistle of an off-tune radio set. The point is that none of these instruments uses as a source of its sound any of the normal strings, pipes or bars, but produces its sound in an entirely new way. As a result of this, the electronic organ can be made to sound either like an ordinary organ or like something completely different.

An elaboration of this is the Melotron, which has built-in tapes of other instruments, so that the player can accompany himself with a complete rhythm section and supporting instruments if he wishes.

In contrast to the foregoing extremely complex and costly instruments are the relatively simple portable or semi-portable electronic organs like those often used in pop groups. They are basically the same as the previous type, but stripped right down to a very few stops, one manual and no pedals, and are light in weight for ease in transportation. They can be played by anybody with a knowledge of the piano.

Further down the scale are the semi-toy instruments, the majority of which look rather like the preceding type but are in fact very close cousins to the accordion, having reeds and chord buttons. Slightly more legitimate is the harmonium, which is still a close cousin of all the others, in having reeds operated by wind provided by pedals, a piano keyboard and several 'stops'. It is the obvious choice of the small church or chapel hall, which cannot run to the expense of a pipe organ.

It is no use trying to give the costs of these instruments. The pipe organs can run into hundreds of thousands of pounds. The modern electronic organs, too, can cost almost anything according to their size and complexity. All the electronic organs except the very largest are easy to play and all can produce excellent music and a lot of entertainment for the player. The small semi-toys, however, must not be thought of as lead-ins to the bigger ones as they have no left-hand keyboard facilities, the bass being supplied by chord buttons.

27 The Harpsichord

The harpsichord was a favourite domestic instrument between 1600 and 1800. It was also an essential part of any small instrumental group. After a lapse of 150 years or so it is now back in favour and many new instruments are being made and played.

The harpsichord has a unique form of sound production. The strings, of which there are now two, three or four for each note, are plucked by a device known as a *jack*—a piece of wood on which is mounted a quill or piece of nylon or stiff leather—which rises as a key is depressed, plucks the string as it goes past and then drops back into place. The harpsichord loses pitch quickly and has to be kept in tune by very frequent attention from a specialist tuner.

The instrument first appeared in Italy in the fifteenth century and early instruments had one set of strings and one keyboard. Later models added the extra sets of strings to produce different tone qualities and stops or pedals to provide combinations of tones. To cope with all this complication an extra keyboard—sometimes two—was added.

Girl playing a sixteenth-century clavichord, which varied from the harpsichord in having its strings set in vibration by brass tangents striking the strings at various points along their length, each string thus being able to produce a number of notes. Later models had one or even two strings per note

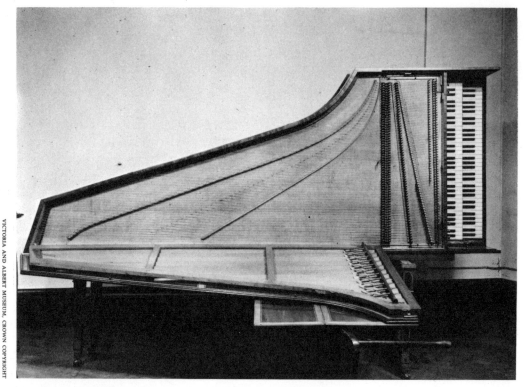

Two-keyboard harpsichord dated 1782, resting on its side with its
lid open to show stringing

The sound is twangy, like a guitar or mandoline being plucked, but unlike those instruments, of course, full chords and running accompaniments are easily produced.

There are various shapes of harpsichord, but the most usual is that in which strings are arranged at right angles to the keyboard which produces a shape rather like a grand piano.

Sometimes the stops were operated by pedals and sometimes there was a 'swell' device that allowed the player to open and close shutters in the body of the instrument to vary the volume. Despite this, however, one of the harpsichord's great weaknesses was that it had very little dynamic range—that is, variation in loudness and softness—and the player could do little to control the expression, unlike the piano, where variation in finger touch has a definite effect.

The harpsichord evolved from the clavichord, first mentioned in 1405, and the virginal and the spinet of the early 1500s, the latter both played by the same plucking method but without the complications of extra sets of strings and stops.

The difference between the last-named instruments lies not only in the simplicity of stringing, but in the shape of the instrument, which in its turn was determined by the way the strings were laid out. The virginal was a mere oblong box, sometimes on its own legs, sometimes just rested on a table. The strings ran crosswise to the player. Virginals were often set one upon the other and known as 'a pair of virginals'. Sixteenth- and seventeenth-century composers loved these instruments and many books of airs for the virginal were published, including the Fitzwilliam Virginal Book, Cosyn's Virginal Book and Forster's Virginal Book.

There is a pretty story that the virginals were named after Queen Elizabeth I, who played the instrument expertly, and who was known as the Virgin Queen. But, alas for the story, the instrument was known by that name before she was born. The name more probably comes from the Latin word 'virga', meaning a rod or jack.

Virginal with lid open
to show stringing, made
by John Loosemore of
Exeter 1655

The spinet was wing-shaped, like a grand piano; as with the virginal the strings run crosswise to the player, but at an angle. Modern spinets can be delightful instruments for a small flat or house where a full-sized piano would be too large, and possibly too noisy. Incidentally one sometimes finds what are described as harpsichords or spinets in the shops of second-hand furniture dealers, but these are almost invariably square *pianos*. In this instrument the strings also run crosswise, but are hit with hammers, not plucked by jacks.

Scarlatti was a great writer for the harpsichord, as was Bach. Couperin wrote graceful tone pictures and Handel used the instrument for lively dance tunes. The harpsichord frequently provides the 'continuo' or general accompaniment in chamber music and choral pieces of the seventeenth and eighteenth centuries.

The revival of interest in the instrument was led by Arnold Dolmetsch who built the first modern instrument in 1896.

In the 1920s Wanda Landowska, a pianist who had for some time been playing harpsichord music on the piano, also took up the instrument and achieved a high standard of playing which encouraged its popularity.

De Falla, the great Spanish composer, has written two distinguished works for the instrument — *Concerto for Harpsichord and Five Instruments* and *El Retablo de Maese Pedro*. Poulenc, the French composer, produced *Concert* Champetre for *Harpsichord and Orchestra* and other distinguished writers followed suit.

The early harpsichordist who accompanied a singer or viol player was not given a fully written-out part to play from, but merely had a guide, showing the tune and the bass notes with figures over them (called a figured bass) and had to make up his own accompaniment as he went along. This procedure was very akin to the way a pianist or guitar player in today's pop groups makes up his own accompaniments from chord symbols.

Another virginal, made by Thomas White, with painted interiors of lid and drop front. When closed it measured $11\frac{1}{4}$ inches deep and was placed on a table for playing

The concertina

Playing position for
the accordion

28 The Accordion

Most people think of the accordion as a comparatively new instrument. In fact, it was invented in Berlin by Friedrich Buschmann in the 1820s, as a development of an Asian free-reed instrument called the *sheng*.

It has the same principle as many wind instruments—a reed beating when an air stream is blown across it. In the accordion, there is a reed for each note and the air is provided by the bellows which are the central part of the instrument.

The right-hand end of the accordion comprises a piano keyboard and is fingered exactly like a piano, with single notes and chords. This piano-style keyboard was not added until the 1850s, all instruments prior to that having only buttons for the right hand.

The left hand plays buttons which, originally playing only single notes, nowadays can play complete chords as well. These chord buttons, which can number up to 120, play three- or four-note chords. The player can tell them apart by the fact that some of them have rounded tops and some have scooped-out tops, so that the player can tell by touch just where the notes are to be found without the necessity of looking at them. Large accordions also have left-hand buttons enabling the player to change tone quality, as on the harmonium and organ. Sometimes these tone controls, called 'tabs', are placed above the right-hand piano-keyboard end.

The instrument works by the player creating wind pressure by pushing and pulling the bellows. The keys or buttons open apertures in a soundboard which allow the wind to play on the particular reed or sets of reeds.

A modern accordion may have 41 piano keys (three-and-a-half octaves), 120 bass buttons (not all different but some repeated for convenience in 'reach'), four sets of reeds, 11 treble tabs (combination stops) and three bass couplers.

But there are many simpler versions, with as few as 22 piano keys and 12 bass buttons. This size is very light and is an ideal instrument for the beginner.

The instrument is normally carried by two straps round the player's shoulders, leaving the hands free to manipulate the bellows and operate the keys and buttons. The player's right hand operates the bellows and plays the melody and his left hand supplies the harmony ready-made from the single bass chord buttons. This is similar to the small electric organs described in Chapter 26.

The pumping of air by the bellows calls for very smooth operation, otherwise the instrument will gasp and splutter. It is also used to give some expression to the instrument—a strong pressure gives a louder note; a sudden sharp stab gives

The melodica, or 'blow organ'

Rumanian accordionist
in a Bucharest café

an accent, and so on. The bellows gives the same note whether pushed or pulled, but if the player wishes to move the bellows without actually producing a note (i.e. at the beginning or end of a phrase, or just to close the instrument at the end of playing), there is an air-release button which allows the free movement of the bellows without actuating the reeds.

There are some variations of the instrument which should be mentioned. The accordion proper has buttons for the right hand, not piano keys, and the bass buttons produce only single notes, not chords. This instrument is often spelt accordeon. Another name for it is the bandoneon. A simplified version, with a dozen or so right-hand buttons and two or four left-hand levers is a melodeon. The 'French' accordion has its reeds tuned fractionally 'out' to give the instrument its characteristic sound. The instrument most generally seen is properly called *piano* accordion by virtue of its piano keyboard, but the term 'accordion' is generally held to mean this instrument and not the all-button version. The slang term is 'squeeze box'.

A close relation of the accordion family is the concertina, but this varies essentially in having single-note buttons at both ends and being hexagonal in shape. It was invented in 1829 by Sir Charles Wheatstone, a physicist. At one stage there were concertinas of various sizes, relating more or less to the instruments of the string quartette, and concert music was performed.

The accordion is very popular where a powerful instrument is required for song accompaniment or dancing. It is fairly easy to play, especially to anyone with a knowledge of the piano, and is readily transportable. There are many accordion clubs which have their own all-accordion bands.

It is a non-transposing instrument and plays directly off piano parts, but the ⎯⎯⎯ must be able to translate the left-hand piano part into chords.

29 The Synthesizer

One of the most fascinating instruments is the synthesizer. Its interest lies in the facts that it produces sound in a way totally different from any other instrument, and that it provides composers with an approach to music which they have never had before.

Electronic music is in a class of its own and must not be confused with the mere amplification of other instruments, nor with just imitating other instruments. Advanced electronic instruments, such as a synthesizer, can do these things but this is not their purpose.

As has been explained earlier in this book, the different sounds of instruments are created by the harmonics, or overtones, that are added to the fundamental

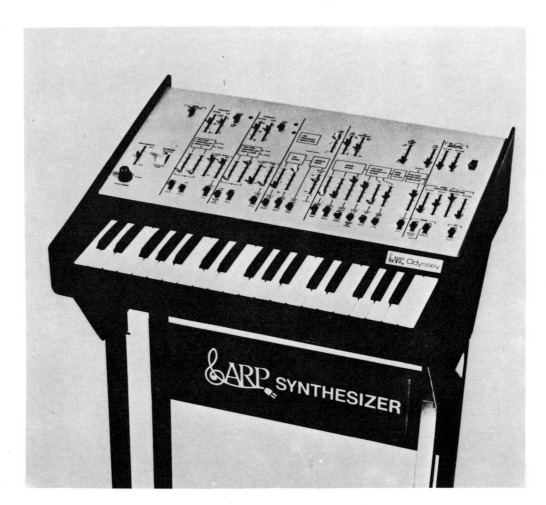

ARP synthesizer

Moog synthesizer being played by Edgar Winter

note. The characteristic sounds not only of instruments but of the human voice and most other sounds is caused by the presence in greater or less degree of harmonics overlaying the 'pure' sound.

Electronic instruments of the synthesizer type work by manipulating these harmonics and 'pure' sounds.

For instance, researchers into electronics found that the recorded sound of, say, a flute, contained certain harmonics and that these harmonics could be stripped off and a fresh set of harmonics added, with the result that the flute recording sounded like the recording of a trumpet.

This is an over-simple explanation of the extreme complexities involved, but is enough perhaps to show that any sound can be literally taken apart and put together again in a different way. This, basically, is the way a synthesizer works. It starts off with a 'pure' tone, and adds harmonics to it—not to make a trumpet sound like a flute—but to sound like something totally new and different, something that never existed before. Hence the term synthesizer—which means 'a device for putting together various parts'.

Using 'generators'—that is, devices for producing sound, which can be vacuum tubes or transistors or other things—the operator produces a 'pure' sound, one without any harmonics or overtones. To this he adds, by means of other generators, any number or kind of harmonics he wishes, to produce any tone, in any scale, of any pitch, that his imagination can invent.

One way of doing this is to produce a 'sine tone' (a pure, bare simple sound) and regulate it in regard to frequency (pitch), wave form (timbre) and amplitude (intensity) and then add any of the hundreds of thousands of tones within the range of human hearing. The permutations and combinations can run into billions. Another way is to produce what is called 'white sound'—that is, a solid wall of noise containing all possible frequencies—and then to filter out what is not required.

Playing a synthesizer, therefore, consists of two stages. First, the required sound is created. Secondly, this sound is used just as it is on any other instrument. The synthesizer has a piano keyboard and (once the first stage is accomplished) is played just like a piano—but, of course, with very un-pianistic results.

Setting up the basic sound or sounds is a highly complicated job and calls for a 'programme engineer'. But, once created, the sound can be reproduced at will by means of tapes, punch cards or other devices.

The musician, after he is satisfied with the tone produced, operates the instrument from a keyboard. He can, of course, have a variety of sounds at his immediate disposal.

The synthesizer has not yet reached the symphony orchestra, mostly because few composers understand it or have written works of stature for it. But *avant-garde* jazz units, and a few very 'progressive' pop groups have made much use of it in recordings.

The synthesizer has not settled into any fixed size, pattern or degree of complexity. Possibly the best known is the Moog (pronounced to rhyme with vogue), developed by Dr R. A. Moog, a PhD electronics engineer from Cornell University. This comes in several models.

Another well-known synthesizer is the ARP. The small portable model has a 37-note keyboard with a seven-octave two-voice range.

One of the shortcomings of the synthesizer in its present stage of development is that it cannot play chords. Soon, however, this will be possible and the range of this instrument extended.

Needless to say, the synthesizer's cost and complication put it outside the reach of the amateur musician. But it has been around long enough (getting on for twenty years) for it to be regarded as a fixture and worthy of consideration by anyone interested in instrumentalism.

Playing position for the
mouth organ

30 The Mouth Organ or Harmonica

The mouth organ, known in America, Germany and some other countries as the harmonica, is a small relative of the harmonium and accordion, both of which work on the same principal of a free reed being agitated by a stream of air. With the harmonium the stream of air is supplied by bellows operated by foot pedals; with the accordion the air is supplied by the bellows operated by the hands; with the mouth organ the air is supplied by the most direct method—by the lungs and mouth.

It has a group of small metal reeds, or

tongues, placed over a corresponding set of holes. The player directs his breath through the holes, thus setting the reeds in motion. Incidentally, the difference between a 'free' reed and a 'beating' reed is that the former vibrates *through* a slot (as in the mouth organ, accordion and harmonium), whereas the latter beats *against* a slot (as in the clarinet and saxophone).

One of the peculiarities of the mouth organ is that each reed gives two tones —one when the air is blown out and another when the air is sucked in.

One of the tricks of playing the mouth organ is to cover the unwanted holes, either with the index fingers or, more usually, with the tongue.

This latter way of playing is quite difficult but is the basis of all 'single note' playing and virtuoso players depend very heavily on this method. Without using it, the mouth organ produces a series of 'chords', changing as the air is sucked in or blown out.

The mouth organ is not new. It came into use in the 1830s and has had a world-wide popularity ever since as an easy-to-play 'fun' instrument.

There are many sizes and models. Some are no bigger than the width of the mouth of the player. Others are large—a foot or more—and have bass reeds. A few genuine 'bass' mouth organs have been made, mostly for use in mouth organ bands, of which there have been not a few. Borrah Minevitch and his Harmonica Rascals, of the mid-1930s, were world famous and produced some quite remarkable ensemble effects.

Chromatic mouth organs, some of which have keys or buttons to make sharps and flats, have also been made. Many of even the cheaper varieties are equipped with a tremolo device.

Some are double-sided—one side playing in one key, the other in another. These have 64 to 96 reeds, with 32 to 48 on each side of the instrument. Usually the keys are C and G.

The usual range is about two octaves, but the chromatic models run to over two-and-a-half octaves in semitones.

The use of the mouth organ is mostly as a solo instrument for simple melodies and easy solos. But there have been a few players who have raised the instrument to a virtuoso level. Foremost among these is Larry Adler, whose wizardry with this simple instrument induced Vaughan Williams to write a *Romance for Harmonica and Strings* for the instrument. In Adler's hands it has become an instrument worthy of ranking with any of the solo orchestral instruments.

It is a matter of interest that the instrument on which Larry Adler produces these remarkable results is not a specially made 'super' instrument, but a standard two-octave factory-produced model such as can be bought in any shop.

The modern method of playing the mouth organ is to cup the instrument in the left hand, and then curl the right hand round the other end, partly to operate the tremolo device, and partly to give it a kind of open-and-closed effect by alternately straightening and bending the fingers.

A device which is favoured by some folk singers accompanying themselves on the guitar is a harmonica holder. This is a gadget which slips over the head round the neck, and holds the harmonica firmly near the lips. The player can sing quite freely and by leaning forward an inch or so, can play the harmonica between singing passages without requiring the use of his hands.

The name 'harmonica' was first applied in the eighteenth century to an instrument which has no connection whatever with the mouth organ, but evolved from the popular trick of rubbing a wineglass round the rim with a moistened finger until it 'sings'. The American Benjamin Franklin produced a kind of mechanical version of this, and both Mozart and Beethoven wrote some pieces for it.

31 The Ocarina, Flageolet and Tin Whistle

These three simple instruments are given a chapter to themselves because they do not fall clearly into any particular category—except that they are all 'wind instruments'—but nevertheless give a lot of amusement to many people and have quite interesting histories.

The ocarina, for instance, is related to a very ancient Chinese instrument called a 'goose egg' because of its shape. The modern ocarina is still more or less egg-shaped with one end sharpened. It is sometimes called a 'sweet potato', again from its shape.

About the mid-nineteenth century the ocarina had quite a vogue in Italy and Austria, where it was made of clay, in two halves, cemented together and baked hard. Today it is often made of fibreglass or plastic. It has eight finger holes, and two thumb holes, and yet another hole from which the sound issues. The mouth-piece, which is built into the instrument, is of the whistle type.

The tenor shawm, a sixteenth-century wind instrument

Its tone is very sweet and mellow, rather like that of a recorder. Its range is rather more than an octave, and it is made in various keys and sizes, although the most common key is C and the usual size is about 6 inches. Its small size, easy technique and pleasant tone make it an excellent 'fun' instrument, in the same class as, but sounding quite different from, the mouth organ.

The flageolet is one of the recorder family and is invariably made of metal. There are various sizes, starting with one pitched in the key of G (the biggest—about 14 inches long), descending through F, E-flat, D, C to B-flat (the smallest—about 9 inches long). With all these sizes available it is possible to play in almost any key and join with the piano and other accurately pitched instruments.

The tone is thin and shrill, very unlike that of the recorder, and because of its very narrow bore, it can only play harmonics. It has a whistle-type mouthpiece and 'speaks' very easily. It has no keys, only holes, of which there are eight—six at the front and two at the back played by the thumbs.

The original flageolet is very old, going back to the mid-sixteenth century, when it was a fashionable instrument played by all classes of the community. In those days it was called the 'little flute', or *flauto piccolo* and became the highest instrument of the orchestra. Eventually it was ousted by the small transverse flute, which kept only the name—piccolo.

The tin whistle is often confused with the flageolet and indeed is similar, both having six holes at the front. In the nineteenth century the flageolet was made of wood and had anything from three to ten keys but today this form of the instrument has completely disappeared.

Like the ocarina, the flageolets and tin whistles are 'fun' instruments, not of orchestral status, but quite capable of producing simple music. Mostly they are played by ear.

One instrument of this class of very great antiquity, which is suddenly having a revival, is the one-handed pipe. This is first cousin to the others but has only three holes, all at the front. It is played with one hand, the player's other hand being occupied in beating a small tabor or drum. It is used in folk or country dancing. The pair of instruments were called pipe-and-tabor, or galoubet-and-tambourine, or even whistle-and-dub!

Teacher and students with home-made bamboo pipes—a form of 'tin whistle'

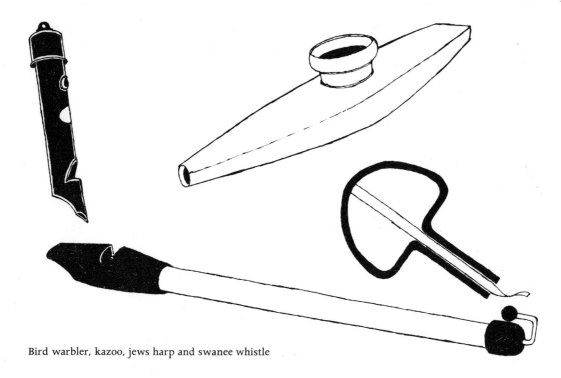

Bird warbler, kazoo, jews harp and swanee whistle

32 Toy Instruments

There is a huge variety of toy instruments, ranging from such ancient devices as the jew's harp, up through kazoos and swannee whistles to a whole group of toy instruments that look more or less like trumpets and clarinets but which are merely reed instruments of the mouth organ type with keys or pistons for each note. Then there are 'blow organs', an elaboration of the same idea, using reeds operated by piano keys, and even simple electronic devices such as the stylophone, which has a small loudspeaker operated by pocket torch batteries and a keyboard actuated by being touched with a metal stylus.

None of these can be described as musical instruments in the orchestral sense, but they all make a simple type of music, are played by ear, call for little or no learning or practice but have their place in interesting young children in 'making music' before proceeding to something a little more difficult.

There is a well-known *Toy Symphony* by Leopold Mozart (often ascribed to Haydn) in which toy instruments are used, accompanied by strings and piano. The instruments are a toy trumpet sounding the note G only, a drum, a rattle, a triangle, a 'quail' bird whistle sounding the note F, a 'cuckoo' bird whistle sounding E and G, and a nightingale warbler. This is good fun to listen to and to watch. The story goes that the composer went to a fair, bought these toys and then solemnly called his musicians for a rehearsal of his new 'symphony', which they couldn't play for laughing! Andreas Romberg and many other composers have also written pieces for toy instruments.

Toy instruments are made in various qualities and at various prices, but are never expensive.

33 The Bagpipes

Of all the instruments about which people make jokes surely the bagpipes gets the worst of it!

And yet it can provide the most thrilling music, as anyone who has heard the pipe bands of the Scottish regiments can testify. And those who have heard a lone piper playing a lament on the ramparts of Edinburgh Castle during one of the Tattoos will know that it is equally capable of producing a sad, longing sound as well.

The first joke to get rid of is that the Scots are responsible for inventing the pipes. In fact, they are known all over the world and have an antiquity of at least three thousand years. They are played by very many races in both Asia and Europe. They probably started in India, whence they eventually percolated to Europe. The Romans played them and carried them to all parts of Europe. There is even a remark in Suetonius, the Roman historian, that suggests it was the bagpipes that Nero played when Rome was burning, not the fiddle.

In France the instrument became a favourite for dancing and from the ninth century it could be found in Ireland. It was not until some three centuries later that it became the national instrument of Scotland.

The original form of the bagpipes was a goatskin bag with two pipes tightly sealed into it—one to blow into in order to fill the bag with air, and the other to let the air out through a series of holes down the front and a tongue-like reed at the end.

Presumably the original purpose of having a bag of air to activate the reed instead of just blowing down the pipe was to avoid breaking the sound by pausing to take another breath.

It was not until the fourteenth century that 'drones' were added. These are extra pipes, each with a reed, and each playing a fixed unchangeable note. It is these drones, playing a continuous chord against the tune, which gives the bagpipes its unique sound.

Originally there was only one drone, then two, three, four or even more. The modern Scottish bagpipes have three drones. The Irish pipes have two, and the Brian Boru version has three—one bass and two tenor.

The principal pipe—the one that plays the tune—is called the chanter and has a compass of about an octave (another

Playing position for the bagpipes

type of chanter has a compass of two octaves and is equipped with keys).

The tuning of the scale played by the bagpipes is unlike that of any other instrument, which is why the bagpipes seldom if ever play with orchestras containing other instruments.

The scale is usually in A major but with a natural G and—most characteristic of all—the C and F tuned half-way between sharp and natural.

Although bagpipes are not used in orchestras their sound has often been imitated orchestrally—usually by playing a simple melody against a 'drone' bass chord of two A's and a D, or two D's and an A. The middle part of many gavottes frequently imitate the bagpipes—a relic of the time when the pipes were used for dancing.

The chanter is sold separately as a practice instrument.

Bagpipe lament on the ramparts of Edinburgh Castle

34 Why Instruments Sound Different in Different Groups

It has been explained earlier in this book that the sounds musical instruments make consist of a combination of a basic, or foundation, note plus a number of harmonics, or overtones, sounding above that note. The presence or absence of these harmonics, and their relative strength or weakness, is what makes the characteristic sound of an instrument.

Even these differences, however, have degrees of intensity. For instance, nobody would ever mistake a trombone for, say, a violin. Yet the high register of the trombone sounds very much like the low register of a trumpet; and the low register of the violin sounds very much like the middle register of a viola, except to the very expert ear.

The Amadeus String Quartet

Acker Bilk and his band

Grouping instruments together, therefore, can have an effect on their sound by merging or covering up some of the instruments' weaker harmonics. This is one reason why composers, when they wish the true sound of a particular instrument to stand out, write a solo for it, with no other instruments duplicating the notes. Another evidence of how grouping instruments together can make them sound different is to be found in what composers call *unison* passages— that is, where a number of instruments all play exactly the same notes. There is, for instance, a quite clear difference between one violin playing a tune and thirty violins all playing the same notes of that tune.

And it is not merely increased volume that makes it sound different—there is a quite noticeable change in tone quality, coming in part from the masking or amplifying of certain harmonics, in part from the slight differences in individual instruments and their players.

The last point—differences in individual players and their techniques—of course has a tremendous effect on how any instrument sounds.

Indeed, one of the pleasures in listening to the master players—and it is easy to compare recordings of the same work played by different people—is to observe the very great differences they produce out of exactly the same instrument.

The author conducting
a recording session—
note 'tools' of the
recording and
broadcasting conductor:
score, stop watch, 'cans'
(headphones) and
talk-back microphone

Roy Wood, in bizarre make-up, at a pop concert

The sound of a brass band is quite distinctive and is unlike any other kind of musical combination even though the brass band includes many of the instruments which are used in other groups. One reason for this is, of course, the total exclusion of any instruments *except* brass. All the sounds are produced in exactly the same way—from cup-mouthpiece wind-blown instruments, all producing the same type of harmonics. With mixed instrumentation these harmonics would be intermingled with the different kinds of harmonics produced by strings and woodwind. And, of course, the instrumentation itself produces the characteristic sound of a brass band.

Methods of playing also make a great difference. For instance, the trombone can be played with a vibrato produced by 'wavering' the slide back and forth (a vibrato can also, but more rarely, be produced by the throat). This gives the instrument a human-voice-like quality which is popular in dance band and jazz units but is rarely used in the symphony orchestra.

This is true of many of the wind instruments—the clarinet, for instance, in the dance band style of playing uses a vibrato (produced by the lips, not by rocking the fingers). Again, in the symphony orchestra, the preferred tone is absolutely unwavering. Occasionally, however, in modern times, there has been a slight tendency to introduce the vibrato into some of the wind instruments of the symphony orchestra, but it is still not common practice—which is rather surprising in view of the fact that a vibrato has always been part of the string players' technique in the symphony orchestra.

This use of vibrato is obviously one of the reasons why instruments sound different in different musical groups, and the potential player should make allowance for it—not only when listening to others play but when he comes to play himself. He will be expected to play in slightly different ways according to what kind of musical group he is playing with.

The first experiments with sounds and their relationships were made around 2,500 years ago by the mathematician Pythagoras, who tried to organize music into a clearly defined mathematical pattern. He got as far as recognizing that vibrations produced sound and that there was a clear and exact relationship between the pitch of the sounds and the number of vibrations, a higher-pitched sound being made by an increased number of vibrations.

The Greeks gave us the idea of arranging music in scales—that is, a series of definite steps with a fixed distance between each step. These were scales of only four notes, arranged in different patterns or 'modes', each pattern being named after a different tribe of people from the West Coast of Asia Minor. They also invented a system of notation based on these scales. Why they picked these particular steps on which to build their scales has not been recorded, but they were almost certainly taken from the way that the songs of the districts were constructed.

Later the theorists came along and measured more accurately the steps between notes and their corresponding vibrations. The eighth (or 'octave'—from *octo*, the Latin word for 'eight') is the most perfect consonance (i.e. agreeable sound) since it duplicates the first note at a higher pitch. The fourth and fifth notes, Pythagoras found, also made harmonious sounds when coupled with the first.

The vibrations of an octave are exactly double those of the foundation note— i.e. A below the treble stave vibrates at 220 times per second and the A within the stave an octave above vibrates at 440 times per second. The half-way mark, E, vibrates at $1\frac{1}{2}$ times the speed of the fundamental—330 per second. And so on.

The Western scale was settled as eight divisions between a note and its octave. But other cultures decided otherwise. In China, for instance, they decided that the most agreeable way to divide up the distance between a note and its octave was in *five* steps, not eight. The Chinese scale is based more or less on our C, D, E, G, A. Incidentally, this is also the basis of Gaelic music in Scotland and Ireland. The Indians took the divisions much more subtly and split the octave into *twenty-two* steps.

The Indians claim that this division into very small steps gives their music a much finer shading and that it can express more delicate nuances than ours. But in dividing this way they sacrificed the possibility of the kind of harmony that can be obtained in Western music.

It is because of these different scale divisions that Eastern music sounds so strange to our ears, which have grown accustomed to our own eight-step division.

Some modern Western composers, however, have sought to extend our range of sound by extending our scales. Schoenberg, for instance, used the twelve semitones in various sequences. The American composer, Partch, invented a 43-tone scale.

All this shows that what our ears have become accustomed to is what we like best. A Chinese child finds our Western music as oddly jarring as we find his. It follows, of course, that his instruments and combinations of instruments would sound very strange to us. Indian music could not be played on Western instruments, nor vice versa, even though the basic principles of acoustics—vibrating strings and columns of air—are identical.

35 The Different Musical Groups

Some instruments, notably the keyboard instruments, the organ, the accordion, and the guitar can be played alone without the help of any others. Most of the rest, however, need to be played in conjunction with other players. The would-be player of any particular instrument, therefore, needs to think a little before deciding to take it up.

Obviously if his taste is to play alone, then he will have to choose one of the potentially solo instruments. A few of the others, such as the violin and the cello, *can* be played without accompaniment, but this is the exception rather than the rule.

There is, however, tremendous enjoyment to be got out of playing with other instrumentalists. Apart from the companionship, there is an infinitely wider range of music available. Moreover, there are many simple orchestral works with which even a near-beginner can cope

quite well, when the strain of being the *soloist* would be quite beyond him.

At the top of the list of musical groups is the symphony orchestra. This is the largest and most prestigious assembly, mostly because its scope and range give composers the finest opportunity to exercise their talents. Without any doubt, some of the greatest musical works have been written for the large symphony orchestra of seventy or eighty instruments. This is not to say, of course, that *all* music written for this type of orchestra is fine and noble—there has been some very bad stuff written as well. But generally this second-rate stuff is played once and then consigned to oblivion.

Then there is the chamber music group. This is the same kind of thing as the symphony orchestra, but smaller. It is composed of almost any combination of instruments and chamber music has been written for trios, quartets, quintets and

BBC Symphony
Orchestra

so on up to twenty or so performers. The instruments, unlike those of the symphony orchestra, can be of any kind or grouping. The term 'chamber music' merely means music intended to be played in a small hall or private room and does not require the space of a concert hall necessary to accommodate a full orchestra.

Perhaps the most popular of small orchestral ensembles is the string quartet —most usually consisting of two violins, a viola and a cello—for which there is a vast repertory.

But there are many other possible groupings—almost any combination of instruments a composer's imagination can conceive. Many of these are based on the piano—piano trios (piano, violin, cello), piano quartet (piano plus string trio), piano quintet (piano plus string quartet), piano sextet (piano, violin(s), viola(s), cello and double bass).

John Philip Sousa, the American March King, 'a man of remarkable personality and musical ability'

Then there are the jazz groups based on the piano—piano, saxophone, trumpet, drums, bass—and many other similar groupings.

In all these the piano provides a solid harmonic background and fills in any missing instrument parts as well as taking the occasional solo.

The military band (called *military* whether it comes from the army, navy, air force or just the local borough council but nowadays more usually called the wind band) is limited to brass, woodwind and percussion. Strings have no real part in it, although occasionally a string bass is included. The particular instrumentation of the military band derives from the marching band, wherein violins, violas and cellos would be impracticable. It also is usually expected to play in the open—parks for instance—where strength and great carrying power are essential.

The range of music played by wind bands is very wide and embraces every kind. Many concert hall works are transcribed for this type of band.

The brass band is first cousin to the military band, but has no woodwind—just brass and percussion. The brass band is found all over Europe, but is probably at its peak in the North of England, which has produced many fine bands over many decades. The competition spirit is very strong in the brass band world and the Annual Brass Band Festival held in London is a tremendous event, with the top-class bands vying with one another before a panel of judges. The quality of playing is very high indeed. The instrumentation varies, but is drawn from various groupings of cornets, flugel horns, tenor horns, baritones, euphoniums, trombones and basses.

Brass bands can and do play almost every kind of music and go out of their way to encourage very young players. It is nothing unusual to see boys (and girls) of seven or eight taking their places in a brass band on any instrument but the very largest basses (even those, sometimes!).

On the lighter side of music the pattern is not so clear. The dance band, as such, has dwindled from a predominance that in the 1930s and 40s meant that there was a band in every one of thousands of dance halls, palais-de-danse, hotels and ballrooms. Its combination was—and still is, where it survives—based on four or five saxophones, four or five brass (two or three trumpets, two trombones) and four rhythm (piano, drums, guitar, string bass). Other instruments were added according to the taste of the band leader —but the basis was four brass, four saxes, four rhythm.

This was the 'big band', mostly too costly to run today except in very large halls or for special occasions. The great bands of the past—Glen Miller, Jack Hylton, Count Basie and many, many others, still exist through their recordings and there are some signs of a revival of interest in the 'big band sound'.

But whereas the dance band limits itself strictly to music for dancing, its modern successor is far more flexible. This kind of orchestra has no definite classification but might be called a light orchestra or concert orchestra. Its instrumentation is extremely varied and includes not only all the standard symphony orchestra instruments but those of the dance band as well, plus any new items such as synthesizers, or brass band items such as flugel horns. It is this kind of orchestra, of anything from twenty to eighty players, calling for extremely high levels of instrumental skill from its players and writing from its arrangers and composers, that comprises the bulk of recording and broadcast music. The Henry Mancini, Mantovani and my own are orchestras of this type.

Then there are the small jazz groups— varying in style from up-to-date imitations of the old-time originals like the Dixieland Jazz Band, through 'middle-of-the-road' and 'trad' groups, to way out, very advanced units that vary very little from the way out, very advanced chamber music groups!

Last, and by no means least, there are the pop groups. Here again there is no set instrumentation, although they are all based on the two rhythm guitars, bass guitar and drums of the Beatles. Today the electric organ and electric piano are frequently to be found in the pop group as well as any of the legitimate orchestral instruments such as the flute, French horn, trumpet and saxophone.

The pop group is without any doubt immensely popular with the young people of all classes and all nations. It has supplanted the jazz groups, the skiffle groups and all other small 'combos' in a fantastic success story that began in the 60s and is far from over.

There is no saying what kind of band will come next—but whatever it is, it will need instruments and players. Even the 'discos' need recordings, and recordings have to be made by live groups.

36 Symphony or Pop?

In the previous chapter we dealt with the various kinds of musical groups—starting off with the symphony orchestra and finishing up with the pop group. It is no part of this book's function to advise for or against either, but it may be useful to note certain facts.

The would-be instrumentalist wants to *play*—that is his sole purpose in learning an instrument. The question is, therefore, where is he most likely to be able to do this and where he gets the most satisfaction? These are not necessarily two sides of the same question.

First, there is the question of instrument. Which is it to be? It may be that the reader has settled this in advance—perhaps because he already has a certain instrument or perhaps because he has his mind firmly made up about what it is going to be. If this is so, then to quite a large extent his choice is already made. The instruments of the symphony orchestra and the pop group are not interchangeable. The piano, however, is—and knowledge of the piano enables one to come to terms very quickly with other piano-like instruments of the pop group —the electric piano, the electric organ and—to some extent—the synthesizer. There is a growing tendency for the pop groups to import some of the instruments of the symphony orchestra and it is possible to find flutes, French horns and other instruments in the pop group. But this is not standard practice—indeed it is the rare exception. To approach a pop group with a violin under one's arm and ask to join in is more likely to be met with astonishment than a warm welcome.

The guitar is not used in the symphony orchestra, except very rarely for some special effect required by a composer.

The drums are certainly used in both types of organization, but in very different ways. The pop group drummer, unless he is a trained musician (and some of them are) would be totally at sea in the symphony orchestra, and vice versa.

So there it is. The 'common' instruments are so few that, with the exception of the piano, the choice of the instrument which you take up, or already have, very largely determines which kind of musical organization you are going to join.

Between symphony orchestra and jazz unit the commonality is just a little greater, though not much. Nearly all jazz saxophone players 'double' the clarinet or flute, which are symphony orchestra instruments although there they tend to be played in a somewhat different way. The string bass is, of course, one of the foundation instruments of the symphony orchestra although in that sphere it depends to a rather less degree on pizzicato (plucking) than it does when forming part of a jazz group. The brass instruments—trumpet and trombone—of the jazz group are also members of the symphony orchestra, although, like the jazz woodwind, they are played in a somewhat different manner.

Drums of the jazz group, however, fall into the same category as the pop group's drums, in having almost nothing in common with the symphony percussionist.

If you want to play the guitar and do not aim at the classical style, you are going to be limited to the pop group or the jazz group, or to folk song accompaniment.

The woodwind go with either jazz or

symphony, but not saxophones which very rarely appear in the concert hall.

The brass similarly—symphony or jazz, but in different styles of playing.

The double bass goes with symphony or jazz but is replaced by the bass guitar in the pop group.

The strings really don't belong anywhere except the symphony orchestra and similar organizations. Occasionally they penetrate to the jazz combination and, very rarely, into the pop group, but they are not very happy away from their classical background.

Finally, then, that all-purpose instrument, the piano. It is equally at home anywhere. If not the actual piano itself, then piano-keyboard instruments. In the very large symphony orchestra it tends to be treated as a solo instrument rather than an orchestral one. But everywhere it has its place, in one form or another.

Right
Two Boys and a Girl Making Music' by Jan Molenaer

37 The Satisfaction of Playing an Instrument

There are some young people who are more or less forcibly taught to play an instrument—usually the piano. Although this happens less and less these days perhaps there are still some suffering under this particular kind of compulsion. A very few of these, perhaps, may survive the early hardships and come to enjoy playing, but the rest will never have any 'feel' for the instrument and the sooner they give it up the better for themselves, their teachers, and all who have to listen to them.

But for the others—those who *want* to learn to play an instrument—a rare satisfaction awaits. There is nothing quite like 'making music', whether it is playing an instrument or singing.

There are hundreds of thousands of players of instruments who will never earn a penny from it, nor reach any level of distinction, who nevertheless find intense pleasure in just playing. First, there is the sheer satisfaction of mastering what is a difficult trick—getting recognizable sounds out of an orchestral instrument. It is not easy to do, as any beginner knows. The painful noises that come out of the first scrapings of a string instrument; the squeaks and gurgles that reward the first tries at a wind instrument —these are enough to discourage all but the most determined.

But suddenly—magically!—a real sound emerges, a musical sound. The first fence has been scaled, the learner has taken off.

From then on it is just practice and then more practice. There is simply no way of avoiding this. There are NO musical instruments—if one excludes the record player and the pianola—that can be played without a lot of initial hard work.

But once the method of producing the right sound has been grasped, the rest comes very quickly, and what intense satisfaction there is in 'the first tune'! Even if it is nothing more inspiring than *Baa Baa Blacksheep* it is a sign of victory, victory over the inanimate piece of wood or metal which has done nothing hitherto but produce awful noises.

From *Baa Baa Blacksheep* to a violin concerto is a very very long road and only the minority will ever make it. But the route is a joyous one, filled with the most delightful stopping places, and however far you travel you are going to find pleasure and much satisfaction.

Many players are self taught, quite a few, having an accurate 'ear for a tune', never learn to read music. There is a lot of pleasure in store even for these people —though the road would be a good deal shorter, even if it seemed stonier at first, if they took lessons.

There are many different kinds of pleasures in playing. Some people never play for anybody but themselves—they are either too shy or too doubtful of their own abilities to want anyone to listen. Nevertheless, they derive much pleasure from their solitary music making, sometimes recording it on a tape recorder and perhaps playing duets with themselves.

Then there are those who join some kind of group. It may be a school orchestra, an amateur symphony orchestra, or a local semi-pro dance band, or a pop group. It may even be a string quartet which is too bashful ever to play anywhere except in the privacy of its members' houses.

But all of these musicians have the pleasure of group activity, of doing something in conjunction with others who are busily doing the same thing. And music is a very collaborative activity —it positively demands participation by others. All great music, except that written specifically for a solo instrument, requires this. And at what is perhaps the other end of the spectrum from 'great music' the drive and excitement of the pop group could not be attained without several people joining together. There is no such thing as the 'one man band'— even the theatre queue entertainer who offers himself as such is really trying to do a job that several people together could do a lot better.

Thus, whether you only aspire to be able to strum a few simple chords on a guitar; whether you intend to join in the playing of great classical works; or whether the peak of your ambition is to be able to play all of the Top Twenty— few satisfactions equal those of playing a musical instrument. Try it and see!

Glossary of Musical Terms

ACOUSTICS	The science of sound.
ALTO	Medium high. The alto saxophone for instance is a high member, but not the highest, of the family.
AMPLIFIER	Electrical device for making sound louder. Used in conjunction with many instruments, especially the electric guitar, which would be inaudible without amplification.
ARRANGEMENT	Strictly speaking the adaptation of a piece of music for a medium other than the one for which it was originally intended. More loosely, the adding of orchestral parts to a single-line tune.
ATTACK	The decisive and firm beginning of a note or passage.
BACH TRUMPET	Small trumpet, pitched in D or E-flat, for playing florid, high-register passages in Bach, Handel, etc.
BAND	Musical group without string players—e.g. brass band, military band, dance band.
BARITONE	Next in pitch below tenor, as in baritone saxophone, etc.
BASS	Lowest pitch of a family—e.g. bass saxophone, string bass.
BASS BAR	Strip of wood in a stringed instrument glued inside the belly, supporting one foot of the bridge under the lowest string.
BASS DRUM PEDAL	Device for beating the drum by means of a foot-operated pedal.
BELL	The flared-out part of the tubing of a wind instrument. Has considerable effect on the tone.
BELL TOWER	Series of hemispherical domes mounted on a central rod. 'Swept' with a wooden drumstick to produce a kind of glissando chime.
BELLY	Upper surface of a stringed instrument over which the strings are stretched.
BONGOS	Small Cuban drums, played with the thumbs and fingers.
BORE	Diameter of the inside of a wind instrument.
BRIDGE	Piece of wood that supports the strings.
CASTANETS	Wooden clappers originally operated by the fingers and thumbs in Spanish-type music, but more usually today mounted on a handle which is shaken.
CHALUMEAU	The name of the earliest type of clarinet, also used to denote the bottom register of a clarinet.
CHORD	Several notes played simultaneously.
CLAVES	Round sticks of wood struck together in Cuban-style music.
COWBELL	Metal bell-shaped device without a clapper, part of drummer's effects, played with wooden snare-drum stick.
DAMP, DAMPER	To check the tone of an instrument: device for doing so.
DULCIMER	Enclosed shallow box with strings stretched over it, struck by hand-held hammers.
EFFECTS	Drummer's extras, such as cockcrow, sleighbells or wind machine.
EMBOUCHURE	The way the lips are formed in playing a brass or woodwind instrument.
ENGLISH HORN	More usually called cor anglais.

FANFARE	Flourish of brass, usually trumpets only.
FIDDLE	Slang name for the violin. Occasionally used as 'bull-fiddle' to describe the double bass.
FIFE	Originally like the piccolo but with no keys. Modern 'marching fifes' have one to six keys.
GONG	Large, circular flat metal plate, producing a deep-toned 'bong' when struck with a padded beater.
HARMONICA	American and German name for the mouth organ. Also an instrument made from domes of glass.
KETTLEDRUMS	English name for the timpani.
LIGATURE	Adjustable metal band used to fasten reeds to clarinets and saxophones.
LYRE	Ancient, harp-like instrument: also metal device for holding music used by marching bands.
MARACAS	Hollow, ball-shaped containers partly filled with small hard objects. Originally vegetable gourds containing dried peas, now more often plastic shells and ball bearings. Shaken to produce a rattle-like rhythm.
METRONOME	Clockwork device for indicating various speeds in music.
MOUTHPIECE	In woodwind instruments, that part of the instrument to which the reed is attached. In brass instruments the cup-shaped device to which the player applies the outside of the lips. Usually of metal, but can be glass, plastic or even horn.
MUTE	Any device that reduces the volume of sound from an instrument.
OPEN STRING	String of a bowed or plucked stringed instrument when not 'stopped' by the fingers.
PIANOLA or PLAYER PIANO	Piano fitted with device that can operate the keys by means of a perforated paper roll turned by pedals or electricity.
PIZZICATO	Plucking the strings instead of bowing them.
POSITION	Where the hand rests on the neck of a stringed instrument—at each separate position a different group of notes lies under the fingers. Also refers to where the slide of a trombone comes to rest.
SCROLL	The carved wooden end of the neck of a stringed instrument.
SLIDES	The short movable lengths of tubing which adjust tuning of a brass instrument.
SOUND POST	Piece of wood fixed inside violins, etc. to counteract downward pressure of the bridge. Important to the tone of the instrument.
SOPRANINO	Highest-pitched instruments.
SOPRANO	Next-to-highest-pitched instruments.
TAMBOURINE	Small, circular one-sided drum with little metal plates, like tiny cymbals, loosely attached round the edge. In pop groups often without the vellum 'drum head'.
TENOR	Next in pitch below alto, as in tenor saxophone.
TENOR COR	Instrument that looks like a French horn but is in fact a member of the saxhorn family: sometimes called a mellophone.
TONGUING	The method of interrupting the flow of wind in playing a wind instrument, either to get a strong attack or to play rapid passages with separated notes. Single-tonguing is represented by the sound *tu*, double-tonguing by the sounds *tu-ku* and triple-tonguing by the sounds *tu-tu-ku*.
TUNING FORK	Device which gives off an absolute correct pitch of one note when struck.

Index